MEMORY IN DISPUTE

MEMORY
IN DISPUTE

edited by
Valerie Sinason

Foreword by
Peter Fonagy

London
KARNAC BOOKS

First published in 1998 by
H. Karnac (Books) Ltd.
58 Gloucester Road
London SW7 4QY

British Library Cataloguing in Publication Data

Memory in dispute
    1. False memory syndrome   2. Psychotherapy
    I. Sinason, Valerie
    616.8'914

    ISBN 1-85575-122-4

Edited, designed, and produced by Communication Crafts

Printed in Great Britain by BPC Wheatons Ltd, Exeter

10 9 8 7 6 5 4 3 2 1

CONTENTS

ABOUT THE CONTRIBUTORS

Dr Gwen Adshead is a Consultant Psychotherapist and Honorary Senior Lecturer in Forensic Psychotherapy at Broadmoor, and was previously Lecturer in Victimology at the Institute of Psychiatry. She has worked as a psychotherapist with both victims and perpetrators of sexual violence. She has researched women with histories of abuse who become violent later in life and is currently working on ethical issues raised by the false memory debate.

Dr Arnon Bentovim is a leading Child and Family Psychiatrist, Family Therapist and Adult Psychoanalyst. A founder member of the Great Ormond Street Child Abuse team, he is currently in independent practice with the London Child & Family Consultation Service, as well as a forensic practice at the private consulting-rooms at Great Ormond Street. He is also continuing research at the Institute of Child Health on the origins of abusive behaviour.

Patrick Casement is a Training Psychoanalyst in the British Society. He is author of *Learning from the Patient* (1985) and *Further Learning from the Patient* (1990).

DR ASHLEY CONWAY is a Chartered Counselling Psychologist. He is Honorary Research Associate in the Department of Psychiatry, Charing Cross & Westminster Medical School. He specializes in trauma counselling in the NHS, Employ Assistance Programme, and private practice. He is the author of over twenty papers and chapters in medical and psychological literature and is currently researching relationships between spontaneous dissociation during or following trauma and hypnotic phenomena.

DR R. D. HINSHELWOOD is a Psychoanalyst and Consultant Psychotherapist and Clinical Director at the Cassel Hospital. His publications include *A Dictionary of Kleinian Thought* (1989), *Clinical Klein* (1994), and *Therapy or Coercion: Does Psychoanalysis Differ from Brainwashing* (1997).

LESLIE IRONSIDE is a Consultant Child Psychotherapist in Brighton, Sussex, having trained in the Tavistock Clinic. He works in the Child and Adolescent Health Service in Brighton, as well as in private practice, and co-ordinates the Child Psychotherapy Lecture Fund in Brighton.

DR JENNIFER JOHNS, formerly a General Practitioner, is a Member of the British Psychoanalytical Society. She has edited *The Ailment and Other Psychoanalytic Essays* (1989) by Tom Main and is joint editor of *Thinking about Children* by D. W.Winnicott (1996). She is presently Chairman of the External Lectures Section of the British Psychoanalytic Society which organizes both introductory lectures in psychoanalysis and events related to the application of psycho-analysis to the arts.

BRETT KAHR is a Senior Lecturer in Psychotherapy at Regents College, London, and Chair of the one-year course in Learning Disability and Psychoanalytic Psychotherapy at the Tavistock Clinic. He works on Dr Eileen Vizard's Young Abusers Project. His book *Donald Winnicott: A Biographical Portrait* was published in 1996.

DR PHIL MOLLON is a Consultant Clinical Psychologist and Psycho-therapist, Lister Hospital, Stevenage. His latest book is *Multiple*

Selves, Multiple Voices: Working with Trauma, Violation and Dissocia-tion (1998). He served on the British Psychological Society's Working Party on Recovered Memories.

DR MARY SUE MOORE is a Consultant Clinical Psychologist and a licensed Child and Adult Psychotherapist in Boulder, Colorado, and an Honorary Senior Psychotherapist in the Child and Family Department at the Tavistock Clinic, London. She was awarded a Fulbright to work with John Bowlby in 1986–88 and worked with Bettelheim in 1977. She specializes in the analysis of children's drawings and the physiology and psychology of trauma, placing a special emphasis on attachment theory. Her book *Reflections of Self: The Impact of Trauma on Children's Drawings* will be published shortly.

SUSIE ORBACH co-founded the Womens Therapy Centre in London in 1976 and the Women's Therapy Centre Institute, a postgraduate psychotherapy training centre in New York, in 1981. Her books include *Fat Is a Feminist Issue* (1976) and *Hunger Strike: The Anorectic's Struggle as a Metaphor of Our Age* (1986), and, with Luise Eichenbaum, *Understanding Women: A Feminist Psychoanalytic Account* (1982), *What do Women Want: Exploding the Myth of Dependency* (1983), and *Bittersweet: Love, Competition and Envy in Women's Relationships* (1988). She writes a column for *The Guardian*.

MARJORIE ORR undertook a Jungian psychotherapy training. She is the founder of Accuracy about Abuse, an international information service providing factual background material on sexual abuse, including abstracts of the latest research. She is a journalist and television documentary producer. A consultant astrologer, she is researching the link between external and internal processes.

PROFESSOR STEVEN ROSE is Director of the Brain and Behaviour Research Group at the Open University. His most recent book was *The Making of Memory* (1994).

ANN SCOTT, formerly managing editor of Free Association Books, is deputy editor of the *British Journal of Psychotherapy* and author of *Real Events Revisited: Fantasy, Memory and Psychoanalysis* (1996), and Senior Lecturer, Centre for Community Care and Primary Health, University of Westminster. Her previous publications include *Olive Schreiner* (with Ruth First) and a collaboration with Mary Barnes, *Something Sacred: Conversations, Writings, Paintings* (1989).

VALERIE SINASON is Director of the Clinic for Dissociative Studies, a Consultant Child Psychotherapist at Tavistock Clinic, and a Consultant Research Psychotherapist at St George's Hospital Medical School, Psychiatry of Disability Department. She specializes in psychoanalytic psychotherapy with learning-disabled children and adults and with sex offenders and victims. She is also a poet and writer, and her books include *Mental Handicap and the Human Condition* (1993), *Inkstains and Stilettos: Understanding Your Handicapped Child* (1994), *Treating Survivors of Satanist Abuse* (1994), *Nightshift* (1996).

FOREWORD

Peter Fonagy

This is a much-needed book—experienced clinicians writing intelligently about one of the most fraught and complex clinical problems facing psychotherapy today.

Researchers writing on this topic often assert the boundaries around the credibility of recovered memory. Cognitive science is well positioned to answer questions about the likely accuracy of memory, the causes of the psychogenic loss of memory, the way that memories are recovered in normal retrieval as well as in assisted retrieval such as psychotherapy, the way that memories are organized in autobiographical memory and how this relates to consciousness, volition, and the self, and the possible psychological effects of memories that are not in consciousness. The boundaries defined by cognitive science are, however, broad. Clinicians have to find their place within it with each of their clients. Knowing probabilities is informative, but such data offer us little about the specific case—only the experience of skilled clinicians can fill this gap. This well-structured and coherent collection of contributions contains a rich reservoir of views on the clinical management of recovered memory.

The title of this volume is, of course, an apt one. While all reasonable professionals will accept the possibilities both of losing access to a childhood experience of maltreatment and of innocent individuals being targeted by illusory "recovered" memories of "victims", the balance between these two possibilities is hard to maintain. There is something akin to a religious war raging between those who wish to protect victims of childhood abuse and those whose declared allegiance is to individuals claiming to be falsely accused. Surely both groups deserve our full sympathy. Surely our concern for the one must not obstruct (or obliterate) our concern for the other. There must be a sensible and thoughtful middle road between extremes, and surely it is unacceptable for anyone who wants to occupy such a position to be accused of betraying one or other of these deserving groups. Yet I fear that this is very much what has happened so far in the 1990s. The objectivity of even the most thoughtful of commentators is clouded by the emotional fervour generated by the issue of recovered memory of childhood sexual abuse and the excitement that is inevitably activated when the gratification of unconscious infantile incestuous sexual fantasies is contemplated. For example, Sutherland, in a review in the Times Higher Education Supplement of Pendergrast's 1994 book *Victims of Memory*, cited an unnamed North American authority claiming that childhood experience had only a marginal influence on adult adjustment.

Others state that the recovery of memory in therapy is inconceivable, as there is no evidence for the repression hypothesis. Kenneth Pope, in a thoughtful review of the field published in the *American Psychologist* (1996), shows how those in favour of the false memory position frequently argue that there is an absence of science on the part of those claiming therapeutic benefits from the recovery of memory, while making unsubstantiated assertions of their own in a manner that can hardly be considered scientific. But there is much that can be legitimately criticized in the publications of those writing with the aim of protecting the adult with childhood experiences of maltreatment. We know too little about the long-term effects of maltreatment in childhood, its critical pathogenic components, and the process of pathogenesis to make clear recommendations about appropriate treatment strategies.

In the meantime, however, we have patients who are suffering—suffering because of memories of experiences with which they cannot cope, with which nobody should have to cope. This book is aimed at the clinicians working with such individuals. For the most part, it does not attempt to resolve the dispute or to provide an illusion of certainty in a context where none can exist. It is a challenge to all of us to preserve precious doubt in a situation where we are under pressure from our clients, from their relatives, and from the general public to adopt a clear position; however, when clarity can only be achieved through extremism, the price is too high—the sacrifice of individual lives is intolerable.

This book contains some excellent chapters, and the editor is to be congratulated on her selection of themes. It is clearly not the final word in the field of recovered memory. It is, nevertheless, an enormously valuable contribution to psychotherapists working within a psychoanalytic framework with an additional impossible dilemma in an already impossible profession.

MEMORY
IN DISPUTE

Introduction

Valerie Sinason

In the past few years in the United Kingdom and America, the concepts of "false memory" and "false memory syndrome" have taken hold of the media and the professional and lay public in a way that requires clinical understanding. There has been an enormous amount of social hurt and heat generated that needs special consideration, as the basic facts are few and are shared.

At the most basic level, everybody's memory is open to question and nearly all of us will have both historically accurate memories and memories that are mixed with fantasy components. So where and what is the problem?

Firstly, these new, untried terms are popularly used only in relation to adults who allegedly recover memories of previously consciously unknown childhood sexual abuse against them. They are not applied in the case of offenders who have committed abuse but have genuinely lost the memory of their corroborated abusing behaviour [Bentovim]. The specific application of the terms makes for complex social and political problems [Orr, Orbach].

Additionally, these adults claiming abuse are mainly women in their 20s, and it is largely their fathers who say that they have a

"false memory". There are cases where women who have left difficult homes with no intention of suing or seeking publicity have
been pursued by fathers who have not accepted their right to leave.
The problem is compounded when such parents, approaching relevant local services using the term "false memory syndrome" as an
entry code, have met with an unprofessional response. Instead of
being listened to with courtesy and sympathy (in that any family
break-up, for whatever reason, contains hurt), supposedly professional organizations have lost their own memory as to who their
primary client was.

The social hurt, heat, need to blame, and consequent lack of
professionalism that has been evoked by this topic therefore needs
to be taken as a lesson. Given the relatively small number of cases
that are involved, the interest generated would suggest [Moore,
Orbach] enormous conscious and unconscious societal terror, such
as comes with a paradigm shift. The gender bias adds to the problems. Freud's early struggle to assess the traumatic aetiology of his
female patients' hysteria returns a hundred years later.

These women are also said to be primarily but not exclusively
in some form of therapy that uses hypnosis, guided imagery, or
other such techniques. This bias can also lead to problems in that
some mainstream workers can sacrifice their "fringe" colleagues to
the media as creators of a new syndrome rather than sharing the
difficulties. Working together is essential, as cases labelled "false
memory syndrome", whether proven or not, provide tragic accounts of individual, professional, and familial pain [Ironside].
Workers and parents are undoubtedly wrongly accused [Ironside],
and to be wrongly accused is to be abused. Why, then, is there
uncertainty and ambivalence about the concept?

To understand the conflict in this debate, we need to see how
the terms were first created. "False memory syndrome" is a term
coined in America by Ralph Underwager and Hollida Wakefield
[Orr] and another American couple, Pamela and Peter Freyd. Together, they had formed the False Memory Syndrome Foundation
(FMSF). The Freyds had (publicly) alleged that their adult daughter had wrongly (privately) accused her father of abuse. The
daughter, Professor Jennifer Freyd, a cognitive psychology expert,
then felt obliged to speak on the matter publicly, although she did

not divulge her alleged core memories. Her uncle, William Freyd, wrote an open letter to a television station in 1995, saying that he, his mother (Jennifer Freyd's grandmother), and his daughters had known that there was severe abuse in the home.

This, of course, does not mean that his words are necessarily correct. However, it does point to the level of familial conflict and dysfunction in the Freyd family and highlights concerns about the social meaning of and response to this topic.

What is the situation like in the United Kingdom? Following a personal invitation, I went to visit Roger Scotford, Chair of the British False Memory Society (BFMS).

I found that we had important areas of agreement. We agreed that memories could become distorted, and that the further back the memory the bigger the problem. We agreed that the problem of child abuse is numerically larger than the problem of being wrongly accused; that to be wrongly accused of abuse is an abusive experience, which can be traumatic and an abuse of justice. We agreed that there is a difference between memory that is recovered and memory that has always been there, that the status of "recovered" memories is very complex, and that the use of hypnosis to recover memories is open to question as it can make a false as well as a true memory appear more confidently.

However, my meeting with Scotford brought to light some difficult ethical issues. Where an allegation involves no witnesses other than the participants, proof is very difficult to obtain. Outside the courts and the consulting-room, there is a further painful no-man's land where the predicament of the alleged victim and alleged abuser is stored. Scotford, like Freyd, reports that he has been accused of abuse by two of his adult daughters. The American FMSF material was the only ray of light he could find to help him understand how these, for him, false allegations could have originated. He founded the British society to help other such parents, and he offers access to BFMS files to bona fide researchers (this is with the permission of the respective parents). In my meeting with him, he offered his own case as an example. This is part of the problem. If Scotford is right and his daughters have made a tragic error, he should be rewarded for his courage in facing up to the issue as well as for his wish to try to maintain or resurrect the relationships. (His relationship with his third daughter has never been problematic.) However, if his two daughters are right and he has abused, his hospitality in providing information could also be seen as exposing their hurt without consent.

However, although Roger Scotford agrees that the main concern is over young women who recover memory of abuse for the first time in therapy, of the 97 British FMS records with adequate information, as seen by the British Psychological Society (BPS) research, only under half revealed memory recovery from total amnesia. It is of great concern that elements in the media have therefore generalized the unproven term "false memory syndrome" [Adshead], referring to alleged memories that were previously unavailable, to extend to all memories of abuse. This takes us from an area where there is at least some consensus (most memories of abuse do remain conscious) to a generalization that ends up being clinically dangerous.

Of course, recovery of verifiable authenticated memory from total amnesia does happen [Adshead, Kahr, Mollon, Moore]. Anne Kelly, for example (*The Big Issue*, 1 April 1996), only remembered that she had borne her father's child at 16 after the birth of her loved daughter in her mid-20s. On searching through medical records, she found proof that she had given birth to a baby boy, who had been adopted. On Tuesday, 26 March 1996, the *Toronto Star* reported that despite the evidence of an expert witness, Dr Harold Merskey, that the complainant suffered from "false memory syndrome", her doctor/abuser was found guilty.

Many such instances are reported. However, great care needs to be taken. The BPS Report (Morton, Andrews, Brewin, Davies, & Mollon, 1995) was particularly concerned about such memories that came from hypnosis, echoed by the Royal College of Psychiatry. Whilst hypnosis can worryingly be used to increase confidence in inaccurate memories in some cases, it can also enhance accurate recall in others. In other words, nothing about the truth or falsehood of hypnotically recovered memory can be assumed without corroborative evidence [Conway].

Individuals with severe dissociative disorders are particularly hypnotizable, suggestible, and fantasy-prone, and they can enter autohypnotic trance states by themselves. This means that memories retrieved through hypnosis or directive methods will contain a confusing mixture of reality and fantasy which requires external corroboration to untangle. Tragically, then, it is precisely those individuals who have been traumatized most who are the most likely to include distortions in their narrative.

Freud used hypnosis at the beginning of his career. However, he was extremely cautious about what could be truly recalled. In the case of Frau Emmy von N (Freud, 1895d), Freud was able to show that even under hypnosis the subject did not have access to the whole extent of her knowledge (p. 98). He pointed out that "It was usually . . . the distaste inspired by the topic which closed her mouth in somnambulism no less than in ordinary life". Freud was also aware that although she was suggestible, nevertheless "I did not make more impression on her in that state than I might have expected to do if I were making an investigation of this kind into the psychical mechanisms of someone in full possession of his faculties" (p. 99). Indeed, promises based on compliance to her therapist "never met with any success". Freud was aware—as is Dr Sandy Bloom, Director of the Sanctuary for Patients with Dissociative Disorders, in the United States (personal communication)—that if patients were so suggestible to their therapists they would get well!

This is not to deny that it is possible to implant a pseudo-memory in someone. Brainwashing is a known and feared phenomenon. However, it would be highly difficult to acquire evidence that a false belief of abuse was implanted, as it is not possible to know for certain that someone has not been sexually abused and it would be unethical to conduct research on this subject [Conway]. Equally, one could then consider whether it was possible to implant a pseudo-memory of non-abuse.

Attachment research has shown that those with good-enough family backgrounds are able to remember positive and negative incidents in childhood, whilst those with more problematic experiences cannot bear to think of any negative experience. "I/they had a wonderful childhood" is the surprisingly common statement of depressed patients and of abusing or depressed parents concerning their children. Could it be [Orr] that a happy childhood is the most common false memory?

Retrieval of memory can be dependent on the cue of smell: "It was the smell of fish and chips and vinegar when I walked past the cafe", said Joan, aged 24. "Suddenly, I was right there back on that stony Sussex beach with my Dad, sitting on a large beach towel, unwrapping my fish and chips. It was a really cold winter afternoon so the chips warmed me up. I was only 4."

For Joan, remembering at the age of 24 a childhood outing with her father, triggered by the smell of fish and chips, there is no problem. One of the ways we know ourselves and our personal histories is through our memories. Indeed, as the BPS report on recovered memories (Morton, Andrews, Brewin, Davies, & Mollon, 1995) made clear, the source of our memories is generally perceived accurately. There may, at times, be partial distortions or inaccuracies. Joan may have correctly remembered that it was cold, but then erroneously thought it was winter because it was cold. However, had that seaside outing been the context of a crime—for example, an act of rape committed by her father—the status and nature of her memory would have to be questioned and such inaccuracies could be legally damaging, regardless of the validity of the core memory.

The moment that a crime is committed and evidence is required and statements have to be taken, the veracity of objective memory becomes of great significance. This is to avoid the further damage of an innocent person being wrongly charged or imprisoned.

Whilst it can be hard enough to date or describe non-traumatic events accurately, the details of time, place, colour, clothes can be even more difficult to recall in the event of trauma. Detailed recall of the traumatic incident alone without such legally important contextual clues may not be evidentially strong. Clinical symptoms as communications are very different to what is required for legal proof. Without an outside witness or adequate forensic evidence, the central core of memory would be in doubt. Language, too, would have to change [Scott]. From possessing a memory, however faulty, Joan would now be legally seen to be in possession of memories of "alleged" facts.

Such a linguistic change can be psychologically difficult. Freud (1933a), for example, writing on the occult, asks the reader: "Permit me now, for the purpose of what I have to tell you, to omit the cautious little word 'alleged' and to proceed as though I believed in the objective reality of the phenomenon." One mother, supporting her child's allegations of abuse against a neighbour, said to me with great shock: "I have been told I could be sued if I speak about 'the' abuse. I have to speak about 'the alleged' abuse. When my house is broken into I can speak about the burglary, but when my daughter is broken into we can't."

Biological change could also occur. At the May 1995 annual meeting of the American Psychiatric Association in Miami, Dr Murray Stein of the University of California, San Diego, and J. Douglas Bremner of Yale University School of Medicine found, independently, through brain-imaging studies, that severe repeated abuse in childhood leads to significant reductions in the size of the hippocampus, which is part of the brain structure that is concerned with memory, especially short-term memory. Women with the smallest hippocampal volume were those suffering most from post-traumatic stress disorder symptoms. Indeed, proven distortion and disturbances in some areas of memory do not rule out the possibility that a specific allegation was true. As organizations like Voice, MIND, and Respond have shown, learning-disabled and mentally ill adults are too often having their testimonies ignored because they are not seen as viable witnesses. Memories of abuse can, in a small number of cases, be delusional. However, this can lead to a dangerous social and professional delusion that psychosis and authentic abuse never co-exist, or indeed to failing to observe that traumatic events can tip a vulnerable individual into a psychotic state. Perhaps the new research of Cicchetti and Tucker (1994) on how early trauma affects neurobiological development will help here.

Had Joan been 9 years old, recounting such a holiday memory, perhaps in the context of a school seaside visit and mentioning abuse, her teacher would have had to follow child-protection procedures. A multi-disciplinary team would then have had the task of evaluating her safety. Children are no longer seen as liars [Bentovim], and research shows that they can have accurate memories of traumatic events. Properly trained clinicians are also more capable of recognizing this and of differentiating between clear and distorted testimony. Research of videotaped sessions with children thought to be abused (Wiseman, Vizard, Bentovim, & Leventhal, 1992) has shown that specialist professionals are far more accurate than others in evaluating the likelihood of abuse and children's statements.

However, the memory of abusers is far less accurate [Adshead, Bentovim, Orbach]. Of one series of 98 children diagnosed sexually abused, 75% of their abusers denied that the abuse had occurred (Hyde, Bentovim, & Monck, 1997), and Trepper and Barrett (1989) refer to a true absence of conscious memory of abusing in some.

Memory of abuse in adults is currently more conflictual than such memories in children. Supposing Joan, at 24, was remembering, or thinking that she was remembering, abuse that took place when she was 9? The English 1980 Limitation Act means that an alleged victim can take to court someone who abused them up to six years previously from the last attack or six years since the victim's 18th birthday. This means that Joan, at 24, would just fall within the legal requirements for taking her father to court, if she wanted to. However, in some American states legal processes are allowed within the six-year period of having a memory of such an event. The repressed is therefore legally allowed to return.

It is fear of the interface of the clinical, legal, and financial (especially in America) that has posed such complex societal, clinical, and ethical problems. Using litigation as an "answer" to tragic family dysfunction rarely works. However, very few of the adult daughters of the members of the BFMS have taken their parents to court [Orr]. Publicly stating that you have been abused is a painful shaming task [Mollon], dealing with secrets [Orbach], and not one that is sought for.

Kay Beaumont, Team Manager for the Maudsley Hospital, London, is concerned (personal communication, June 1995) that, regardless of whether memories are or are not retrieved and whether therapists are good or bad, there has been little attention paid to the way in which some parents assume the right to exert control over their adult daughters by influencing the therapy that they receive and demanding parental contact despite their daughters' wishes. "Such parents appear unable to accept that their daughters can speak for themselves, and the idea of a therapist who is as controlling as they are begins to make sense for them. If they have lost control of their daughters, then someone else must be exerting influence over them. The possibility that a daughter is assuming control for her own life cannot be contemplated."

Hence, in Newcastle upon Tyne, there was a need to create DATA (Daughters and Their Allies: see Appendix), a campaign to protect such women. In fact, it was founded, in July 1994, to support the first woman in Britain whose father's defence team had mobilized false memory syndrome against her evidence that he had raped her throughout her childhood. She had never forgotten her abuse.

There is historic truth [Rose], which actually happened, and narrative truth, a person's account of a remembered experience; or, where adult patients are concerned [Adshead, Casement, Johns], there is the major difference between objective fact, which is provable and is a concern of the courtroom, and psychological truth, which is the concern of the consulting-room.

Freud tried to make a bridge between these two worlds. In June 1906, at the request of Professor Löffler, Professor of Jurisprudence, he gave a lecture at the University of Vienna on psychoanalysis and the ascertaining of truth in courts of law. He began, expressing the surprisingly topical concern, "There is a growing recognition of the untrustworthiness of statements made by witnesses, on which, nevertheless, so many convictions are made" (Freud, 1906c). He drew an analogy between the work of the therapist and the work of the court: both were concerned with a secret, and both were having to uncover hidden psychic material. However, they used different detective devices.

Importantly, he pointed out that forensic word-association tests could be problematic outside experimental or clinical situations, because someone innocent could act as if he or she were guilty. Current research [Bentovim] shows that the reverse is true—that guilty people can act as if they were innocent. In a very cautious way Freud recommended, therefore, that such testing should be undertaken for a fixed number of years without the results being allowed to influence the court. Then a proper research evaluation of the findings could be undertaken. However, he was very aware that tests needed to be made on real subjects, as experiments would be "dummy exercises" (p. 114) that could not offer actual practical application—something that many of the false memory experimenters would do well to learn.

Indeed, experiments done with volunteer subjects cannot help us to understand traumatic memory [Mollon, Moore]. If an individual is asked to recount a specific event in different moods or places, recall will vary because the context in which memories are retrieved is part of the memory itself [Moore, Mollon, Rose]. I have a painful clinical example. When working with a traumatized patient who, in a trance-like state, was recalling being covered with paraffin and threatened with a lighted match, I was shocked to see her change colour and start choking. I said: "And I am next to you and I am throwing water over that fire to put it out." Slowly, her colour returned, she stopped choking, and, to my great relief, she came out of her trance. A few weeks later, when she was in a similar state reliving the incident, her colour suddenly returned to normal and she announced that someone there was rescuing her, pouring water over the fire. She was quite right. She had an accurate memory of what I had said to her. However, due to her mental state, my words had taken on physical properties.

Patients in these mental states, who have been traumatized, are more vulnerable to having both true and distorted memories coinciding. This means that an area of intellectual doubt is required as well as an empathic response.

Freud took care always to keep an area of intellectual doubt in his mind. When dealing with a patient (the Wolf Man) whose disturbance seemed to have possible links with witnessing a primal scene, Freud (1918b [1914]) commented: "I intend on this occasion to close the discussion of the reality of the primal scene with a *non liquet*" ("It is not clear"—a verdict where the evidence in a trial is inconclusive). It is crucial for therapists and psychoanalysts to keep this area of doubt. With a certain number of adults there will always be uncertainty as to the validity of memories, and the task of the therapist [Casement, Johns] is to manage that uncertainty. Not knowing can be painful. Where the evidence for validity builds up [Adshead, Johns, Mollon, Orbach], knowing is painful.

In chapter 9, Steven Rose points to the need for careful training and registration to deal with this. Cesare Sacerdoti, publisher of

Karnac Books and the original impetus behind this book, worries
about intrusive therapy: "There is not enough clarification as to
who is supposed to be allowed to be a therapist, and that is one of
the weaknesses in the profession. A doctor is a doctor, and even
there you get problems. But if you have a surgical team, people can
intervene if the surgeon is wrong; but if a therapist is wrong, no-
one can. When two people in therapy are present at the same
happening, what causes the overlapping or difference between the
two circles in terms of memory? When you come to a fine-tuning
of the memory, you can understand why the other has remembered or experienced something different. I am concerned that
where this does not occur there has been faulty or intrusive
therapy" (personal communication).

Indeed, R. D. Hinshelwood subtly points out in chapter 12 that
a "false" memory of the past can be a representation (distorted) of
a true perception of the present (with an intrusive therapist) or a
true memory of some event that was falsified in the past.

Psychotherapy in the United Kingdom is only just becoming
accountable, with the British Confederation of Psychotherapists
(BCP) representing most of rigorous psychoanalytic psychotherapy trainings and the United Kingdom Council for Psychotherapy (UKCP) as the largest umbrella organization for almost all
trainings. Poor practice in any profession needs attention. However, isolating one form of treatment for scapegoating, rather than
as part of a general genuine wish to improve mental health training, is also dangerous, as is the damage to health from some mainstream clinicians who may have a bias towards not recognizing
abuse.

As I have stated elsewhere (Sinason, 1997), within the trained
non-directive psychoanalytic community the greatest problem
concerning abuse, as both Alice Miller (1985) and Jeffrey Masson
(1984) have pointed out, has historically been the inability of the
therapist to hear it rather than the direct implantation of alien
ideas. Indeed, within the United Kingdom up to ten years ago only
a very small number of psychoanalysts within the Health Service—such as Drs Arnon Bentovim, Mervin Glasser, Brendan
McCarthy, Judith Trowell, Eileen Vizard, and other colleagues—
had dealt with issues of abuse and abusing.

Additionally, those who have a vested interest in discrediting the testimony of genuine abuse survivors are not stopping at the fringe door. Those who use carefully learned hypnotherapy skills for the benefit of deeply disturbed patients (including medically approved abreactions) are in danger of being confused with true or imaginary (caricatured) stage magicians, tunnel-visioned abuse zealots, and simplistic, directive, but well-intentioned therapists with no knowledge of different kinds of memory.

Psychoanalysis [Hinshelwood, Kahr] was founded on theories of memory. These theories can be extremely painful to consider. For example, one other important kind of remembering that Freud elucidated is the memory that comes through unconscious repetition and re-enactment. The nature of a difficult birth, pre-verbal trauma, and childhood trauma [Johns, Mollon] can find a way of being bodily re-enacted in drug addicts (as Dr Earl Hopper, 1995, has shown) and experienced in the transference and counter-transference [Hinshelwood, Johns, Mollon, Orbach]. Whilst Mary Sue Moore (chapter 13) can show the way that early experiences are re-enacted without cognitive representation, our lack of conscious remembrance of these days involves us having to trust in our parents at a most vulnerable time in our lives.

Children's playground games often include blindfolding. There is an evaluation of how much the individual has reason to trust the group. What can happen to someone who is not able to see what is happening? Walking up the stairs at night without a light on is also a frightening experience to many children (and adults). The fear can be of haunting oneself with internal ghosts, or it can be a remembering of being "in the dark" about a variety of events. Often at the basis of our concern at infantile amnesia is our adult anger that we are not in control of our minds—our unconscious or, indeed, our first few years.

With the therapeutic relationship, a patient transfers to the therapist a verbal and non-verbal re-enactment of such early scripts. These take time and training to understand. In the *Lancet* (16 October 1965, pp. 785–786), psychoanalyst Dr Anne Hayman brilliantly explains why she could not break confidentiality to speak in court. The point was made that it could take years to understand what was said in the consulting-room and that there were enormous professional dangers in treating anything said as if it were part of "normal social interchange". She concluded that if something the patient said was to be treated as objective evidence, it would be necessary to prove it by explaining all the known underlying meanings: "Justice, as well as our ethic, is best served by silence."

In most cases, this is undoubtedly true. Psychoanalysts and psychoanalytic psychotherapists are primarily (or even totally) concerned with a patient's emotional truth, regardless of whether or not it is corroborated by external reality. However, some of us (Hale & Sinason, 1994) consider that where an actual serious legal offence is being discussed [Ironside], the real event needs to be objectively examined and validated (or ruled out), where possible by someone who is not involved in the therapeutic relationship— preferably a police officer. Indeed, we have just completed a Department of Health–funded research project at the Portman Clinic to see what external corroboration is available for allegations of ritual abuse, in terms of both checking the validity of other facts in the patients' lives to see whether there is any underlying delusional system and making police links. This work is continuing at my Clinic for Dissociative Disorders.

Within the field of adult learning disability (Hollins & Sinason, 1993, 1994) and child protection—with the work of psychoanalysts Arnon Bentovim (1992), Judith Trowell (1986), and Eileen Vizard (1988), and organizations like Respond, Napsac, and Voice—the making of a bridge between treatment and the courts has aided social justice and internal improvement. Within the field of individual adult treatment, we are (as Mollon points out in chapter 10) damned if we listen and damned if we do not. We need to keep our minds open and try to hear and treat the social hurt.

There are some adult patients [Casement] who have a vague sense of unease as to the possibility of abuse and who may have come from emotionally unboundaried families, and I have worked with some of these—even showing that abuse did not occur (Sinason, 1997). Such families require treatment to deal with the consequences of the allegation and to work on the family dysfunctions that have often led to it. A detailed analysis of the nature of such dysfunctions [Casement] would be useful in the future. However, support in both the United Kingdom and the United States for such small numbers is enormous compared to the disconfirming and discrediting of the tragically large number of abuse survivors. Those who bear the physical and mental pain and the corroborative medical evidence that abuse has occurred may receive little justice (Sinason, 1994), for the law has to be concerned with who can be proven to have done what to whom—not to confirm whether or not something has happened. All too often we confuse these two issues.

Memory—for evolutionary purposes—is largely accurate [Moore]. So is memory of trauma. Whilst the consulting-room deals with myriad layers of memory and fantasy, we should not forget the larger canvas. In protecting the complexity of internal reality, we can be doing a disservice to some of our patients if we fail to recognize the external.

Formally trained psychotherapists are very aware that the meaning of truth is a complex one. Psychoanalytic psychotherapists are also aware of the different status of direct and repressed memories and the vulnerability of those in traumatized states. However, that can make some of us far too uninvolved in checking the damaging growth of the "false memory syndrome" concept. It is very difficult for genuinely innocent parents whose children have accused them of abuse to realize that their understandable grief and anger has, in some cases, endangered the treatment and lives of the tragically many more families where abuse really has gone on. The consulting-room is not a courtroom, but by avoiding the meaning of external legal aspects we risk patients' health and professional freedom.

Accusing a therapist of implanting a false memory of abuse is a new form of something we understand very well: it is another version of asking how a child abuse case was "handled", instead of asking how the children are. In other words, it is a displacement. The professional becomes the unwanted messenger of abuse who can be publicly attacked, whilst the dynamics that lead to a frightened adult saying that she has been abused (whether correctly or incorrectly) get lost. We need to remember that the waters of forgetfulness were the waters of Lethe. Forgetfulness in professionals can indeed be lethal and more dangerous than remembering.

The painful dynamics of this subject are played out at every level within the media and the professions. Some sections of the media seemed not to realize that the Royal College of Psychiatry's Working Party Report was not viable in its initial form.

As Professor John Morton, the Head of the BPS Working Party on Memory, saliently pointed out (Personal Space, *The Psychologist*, 1998, p. 408), half of the six members of the Royal College of Psychiatry Working Party had longstanding connections with the British False Memory Society. As the Forensic, Child & Adolescent & Psychotherapy Sections of the College criticized the report, in addition to one member of the working party, the Royal College declined to publish it and the flawed "Brandon Report" was published separately.

Perhaps the only ray of light is the shared overall agreement between the original working party, the British FMS, and the BPS of the significant figures of abused children and adults, the strengths and vulnerabilities of memory, and the pain of being wrongly accused.

My views in this introduction are my personal ones and may not be shared by other contributors to this book. However, what is shared is the hope that the human tragedy involved in traumatic memories—whether true or false, whether expressed by victims or perpetrators, by children or adults, by those with learning disabilities, mental health problems, or chronic dissociative states—will be listened to with the courtesy it needs and deserves.

CHAPTER ONE

Flying by twilight: when adults recover memories of abuse in childhood

Gwen Adshead

In this opening chapter, Gwen Adshead provides a careful overview of the research literature concerning the main issues in this debate. She includes legal issues and child and adult memory in her remit.

"Suspicions amongst Thoughts, are like Bats among Birds, they ever fly by Twilight . . . In Fearful Natures, they gain ground too fast."

Francis Bacon

T he delayed recovery of war or POW experiences by army veterans many years later appears to have gained some public and professional acceptability. However, when this same phenomenon of recovery is described in relation to memories of child abuse, this has caused controversy, both in the lay public and within professional groups (Berliner & Loftus, 1992). Polarized positions have been taken up by professionals asked to adjudicate between adults alleging abuse and other adults denying it. Claims of abuse based on recovered memories may lead to

17

family disruption and distress and, infrequently, to legal charges of criminal assault or suits for compensation (Loftus, 1993). It is suggested that such claims are most frequently made in the course of psychotherapy and have been associated with the use by therapists of hypnotic techniques.

Psychiatrists, psychologists, and other health care professionals may be instructed, in legal cases that may arise following such allegations, to give expert witness about memory, child abuse, psychotherapy, dissociation, and trauma, *inter alia*. However, the breadth and validity of the information base available for expert witnesses to draw upon is still uncertain. To date, there are very few systematic studies of the nature of these claims of recovered memory, nor of the people who make them. The media has dubbed such claims "false memory syndrome", but such a "syndrome" is not described in databases of psychological literature. It may be helpful to take each of these terms in turn.

False

The word "false" may imply several interpretations. One of these is that, in any particular case, the claim is false because childhood abuse rarely occurs. This argument appears hard to sustain. At least thirty years of research and clinical description has established that childhood abuse does occur, and that abuse is most frequently carried out by parents, step-parents, or trusted adults. Two English community prevalence studies found similar figures for the prevalence of child sexual abuse, with between 9% and 12% of the adult population reporting an experience of sexual abuse in childhood (Baker & Duncan, 1985; Bifulco, Brown, & Adler, 1991); this is half the rate of neglect or physical abuse. It is therefore not unlikely that a minority of the adult population will have true memories of being abused as children. There are many types of abuse, and it is of interest that "false" memories have only been associated with claims of sexual abuse.

Subsumed under the category of "false" are two further interpretations. One reads "false" as "maliciously untrue", the implication being that claimants are fabricating memories to get their childhood caretakers into trouble, because they have a grievance (ACAP, 1993, p. 2). Although this is commonly alleged, there is currently no evidence either to support or to refute this interpretation. The literature on false allegations of abuse made by *children* (not adults) suggests that malicious allegations are very rare (Adshead, 1994). At present, there are no studies of adults that confirm or refute that adult survivors of abuse commonly make such malicious allegations. There is some anecdotal evidence that people who experience such memories are genuinely distressed (Loftus, 1993), and this distress is exacerbated by parental denial or family dispute. In this author's experience of working as a therapist with both adult survivors and perpetrators of child sexual abuse, there appears to be little evidence of adults in triumph over their parents' discomfiture, or gleefully pursuing them to court. Most adults presenting with uncertain memories of child sexual abuse have been just as distressed as their families by the ensuing discord and the loss of attachment to all family members.

It has been suggested that false claims of abuse have led to a huge increase in the number of such cases being raised against alleged offenders. However, examination of criminal statistics does not bear this out. A search in Massachusetts law library for the number of cases over the last three years of alleged child sexual abuse based on recovered memories found only five cases (van der Kolk, 1994). There are no equivalent English studies; however, in England and Wales, the number of incest convictions in 1993 was identical to the number in 1946, and the number of convictions for indecent assault has not altered greatly over the last ten years (Home Office, 1994; Walmsley & White, 1979).

To date there are no scientific descriptive studies of subjects whose memories of child abuse have been shown to be false. There are clinical accounts of *retractions* of allegations, and accounts of legal cases where allegations were not pursued or convictions not obtained. But these cases must be set against the fact that only 11% of *all* indictable offences result in a criminal charge or summons (Home Office, 1994). In cases of adult rape, for example, the conviction rate is more like one in ten (Mawby & Walklate, 1994). It therefore seems very hard to conclude that there are huge numbers of new cases of sexual assault resulting in wrongful convictions.

A second interpretation of "false" suggests that such memories are not "real" and would imply that it is the nature of the memory itself which is false. In cases of "false memory", there is a confusion about the truth, where it is argued that the victim mistakenly believes in the abuse, as a result of experiencing a memory that is "false". It is this that will be discussed below.

Memory (i)

Over the last ten years there have been accounts, followed by empirical study, of "pseudo-memories" induced by hypnosis (Laurence & Perry, 1983). The "pseudo-memories" usually consist of false information given to laboratory subjects while under hypnosis, by the experimenter, who induced hypnosis. Pseudo-memory acquisition is most likely when information is introduced about a memory acquired a long time ago, but retrieved only recently (Gudjonsson, 1992). There is debate as to whether the pseudo-memory replaces the original memory, or co-exists with it (Gudjonsson, 1992). The misleading information is usually fragmentary and trivial, rather than central to the individual, although it has been suggested that quite complex new information can be introduced (Loftus, 1993).

This research into the formation of "pseudo-memories" under hypnosis has had a particular influence on legal proceedings, when hypnosis has been suggested as a way of retrieving memories of witnesses. Scepticism about the reality of such memories in terms of evidence has lead courts to be cautious about, or even refuse, the introduction of such evidence (Loftus, 1981; Orne, 1979).

Despite legal scepticism about the use of hypnosis as evidence in the courtroom, the therapeutic use of hypnosis has continued and has been advocated particularly with those patients who are thought to have repressed memories of childhood trauma. This approach is based on the theory that the successful treatment of post-traumatic stress disorder (PTSD) requires the recall and cognitive processing of traumatic memories. Such treatments have been developed and studied principally in patient groups who have survived trauma in adulthood, such as war or major disasters. It is not clear to what extent such treatments are indicated for patients who experienced trauma in childhood. It is also not clear whether such treatments are efficacious when memories of trauma are not accessible, or where the existence of trauma is supposed but is denied or not considered by the patient. Nevertheless, it is accepted practice for therapists working with incest and child abuse survivors to use the same PTSD model. Where there are clear memories of childhood trauma, this therapeutic approach is described as successful (Sgroi, 1989).

Can therapists using hypnosis implant memories? None of the studies of pseudo-memory implantation, nor of the effect of hypnosis on legal testimony, have been carried out in *clinical* settings. However, some research findings from laboratory studies of pseudo-memory implantation under hypnosis may suggest how memory implantation might be possible in a clinical setting. Easily hypnotizable subjects are more likely to report false memories (Barnier & McConkey, 1992; Laurence & Perry, 1983; Sheehan, Statham, & Jamieson, 1991). Contextual cues can make reporting of false memories more likely (Spanos, Gwynn, Comer, Baltruwiet, & de Groh, 1989). Some workers believe that pseudo-memories represent response bias in an effort to answer questions asked by the hypnotizer, and that pseudo-memories can be reduced by providing motivation to give accurate answers (Murrey, Cross, & Whipple, 1992). An interrogative style of therapy might produce false material, as happens in those who make false confessions (Gudjonsson, 1991).

Studies of adult survivors of childhood abuse show that they may be over-compliant with other adults whom they perceive as powerful, such as their therapists (Kluft, 1990). Some types of therapy encourage dependence, which increases the power of the therapist. It could be argued that the therapist who imposes any line of questions, technique, or theoretical stance is at risk of unconsciously (or consciously) taking advantage of patient compliance. Patients may then seek to "please" the therapist by producing material that seems to be sought, producing a form of psychodynamic "response bias".

The prevalence of patients with sexual abuse histories in a clinical population is likely to be higher than in the community at large, thus distorting the perspective of both clinicians and researchers. A history of childhood sexual abuse increases the risk of psychiatric caseness in adulthood, a risk that increases with the severity of the abuse (Bifulco et al., 1991; Mullen, Martin, Anderson, Romans, & Herbison, 1993). It is therefore not unlikely that some vulnerable patients, exhibiting psychological distress, will recall sexual abuse in childhood. A combination of a distressed individual, who may be suggestible, with an interrogative style of therapy, may set a scene where there is at least a risk of pseudo-memory formation—*regardless* of whether there is a true history of childhood trauma.

Memory (ii)

Those who support the notion of "false memory" argue that most people who have experienced childhood trauma have clear memories of this, and no difficulty of recall. However, there is research evidence to suggest that this is not true of all survivors. In one study of sexually abused women, 19% had total memory loss for the abuse during some period of their lives, while another 12% had large memory gaps (Loftus, Polonsky, & Fullilove, 1994). In another study of 440 subjects who remembered an experience of sexual abuse, 56% reported partial amnesia for the abuse at some time in their lives (Briere & Conte, 1993). In a seventeen-year follow-up study of 129 women with *documented* histories of childhood sexual abuse, 38% did not remember having been abused (Williams, 1994a). Such traumatic amnesia may be understandable as a neuropsychological phenomenon which is part of the response to chronic trauma, rather than a result of psychological mechanisms such as repression (van der Kolk & Saporta, 1993). It appears, therefore, that it is not uncommon for some survivors of childhood trauma to have incomplete memories of their experiences.

A related argument suggests that memories recovered in therapy may be distorted by psychiatric conditions, such as mood disorders, making recall of unpleasant events more likely. However, studies of the effect of mood on memory have suggested that although mood may make it harder to remember good events, it does not ease access to bad events (Brewin, Andrews, & Gotlib, 1993). Similarly, there is no evidence that people with mood disorders recover new memories, but they may, rather, distort old ones.

It is often suggested that therapists and researchers into child abuse do not attempt to obtain independent verification. Such verification is sometimes possible, and sources may be offered by patients or relatives. One study of recovered memories of abuse in therapy found that there was independent verification of all the abuse histories (Herman & Schatzow, 1987). A more recent U.K. study of child abuse in the community found that other family members confirmed histories of abuse given by subjects (A. Bifulco, personal communication; for methodology of this research, see Bifulco, Brown, & Harris, 1994).

Therapists who have been involved in "false memory syndrome" cases are said to be directive in style and militant in philosophy, and are also said to advise patients to confront abusers or bring legal action. There is little published evidence to support this view, which appears to be based on a criticism of the child abuse literature rather than an empirical study of therapeutic style. In one study of sixteen therapists who had seen a case of "recovered" memory of abuse, 81% believed their patients' accounts (E. Loftus & C. Herzog, unpublished data, cited in Loftus, 1993). The authors suggest that this willingness to believe patient accounts of recovered memories may reinforce what may be only suspicions or uncertainties. A difficulty with such an argument is that health care professionals are not trained to be sceptical about their patients' accounts of themselves. Therefore, it is not surprising that therapists believe what they are told by patients. If this were to change, it would be a radical change for most health care professionals.

To date, much of what has been written about so-called "false" memories has been obtained from expert testimony within legal proceedings, or from newspaper accounts. In a recent article in a scientific journal, fifteen out of twenty-eight references are obtained from newspaper articles, and twelve are from legal cases (Matasar, 1994). Although this material may reflect public concern, neither the law courts nor newspapers are arenas for scientific enquiry, where evidence for and against hypotheses is assessed and scrutinized, and presented in a balanced way. For example, real concern that over 200 families have joined the British False

Memory Society needs to be set against concern about the 100 convictions for incest and over 3,000 convictions for indecent assault each year in England and Wales.

Syndrome

By definition, a syndrome refers to a group of clinical signs and symptoms, indicating an underlying pathology, which may be as yet unknown. The popular media, by using this term, may give a spurious clinical significance to that which may have its roots in some other cause. A sense of empiricism is given to something that may as yet be a completely random collection of observations, contaminated by sampling and observer bias.

One of the difficulties for researchers and clinicians in evaluating the evidence about "false memory syndrome" is the lack of rigorous scientific descriptive data about the phenomenon, obtained in the setting in which it is said to occur. For example, information based on laboratory studies of healthy volunteers may not easily generalize to clinical settings. Much of the evidence appears to have been generated in the context of a small number of legal cases, where experts are required to be partisan. No serious scientific enquiry could be based on courtroom evidence, where it is not possible to control for a huge number of human variables which affect data collection and interpretation.

It is also clear that adversarial legal systems have very different theoretical and philosophical approaches to the establishment of fact, when compared to the traditional empirical approach of clinical medical science (Eastman, 1992). In a recent case where scientific views conflicted, the U.S. Supreme Court in *Daubert v. Merrell Dow* offered three possible criteria for the admissibility of expert evidence (Bertin & Henifin, 1994):

- Has the theory been tested, published, or subjected to peer review?
- Is the theory generally accepted?
- What is the known rate of error?

If these criteria were applied to the current state of knowledge about "false memory syndrome", it is hard to see how any expert evidence could be admissible, given the current state of scientific information about the incidence of this phenomenon, its cause, or its effects.

In empirical terms, investigation remains at a very early stage. Detailed descriptions of the phenomena in uncontaminated settings, made by impartial observers, are lacking. In addition, the debate has been fuelled by impassioned statements by those who claim that all such memories are false, and those who claim that they are all true. Such statements do not constitute a scientific description of a phenomenon that might prove, with investigation, to be a syndrome. Statements like "[this piece on FMS] was so 'balanced' that it was difficult to pick out the arguments" may give an indication of the strength of feeling that drives and polarizes the debate (ACAP, 1993, p. 4).

A particular difficulty in applying a traditionally empirical approach to this phenomenon is one that is common in forensic psychiatry: namely, that the behaviour under discussion is an alleged crime. Forensic psychiatrists and psychologists are very familiar with clinical situations where offenders and victims offer different versions of events, and it is common for alleged offenders of all types to accuse their victims of lying. Protestations of innocence are particularly prominent in child abusers, and many, if not most, offenders deny offending, even after conviction (Abel, Mittelman, & Becker, 1985; Kennedy & Grubin, 1992). Denial is clearly no sign of guilt but, equally, no sign of innocence. Attempts to determine some scientific truth based only on the statements made by either the alleged victim or the alleged perpetrator are likely to fail.

Traditionally in Anglo-Saxon jurisdictions, allegations of crime are investigated by law-enforcement agencies and proved or disproved in a court. The veracity (or otherwise) of allegations is not decided by mental health workers (or, indeed, by any other sort of health care professional), who have no expertise in truth detection (Becker & Quinsey, 1993).

If therapy-induced pseudo-memories did appear to be clinical in origin, then this might be related to a number of clinical factors that could be investigated empirically. In relation to individual patients, it might be asked why there appear to have been very few reports of "false memories" in male survivors of sexual abuse or in survivors of physical abuse. In relation to therapists, it might be possible to investigate whether it is true that certain types of therapeutic style are over-represented in cases where memories are said to have been implanted.

In relation to therapeutic interactions, one question might be whether it is really therapeutically essential to access all memories of any trauma, before therapeutic work can begin. Many distinguished psychotherapists, including Freud himself, have suggested that there is no indication for forcing patients to remember traumatic events (Briere, 1993, p. 136; Freud, 1913c). The patient who comes for therapy may have other problems that are not directly related to childhood trauma. There are many reasons, apart from childhood trauma, why adults may become psychologically distressed. Childhood experiences may be relevant, but not causal, nor primary.

Conclusion

Before stating (inevitably) that research is necessary, the first question is whether all the relevant questions can be the subject of research, in the traditional medical sense. Another reading of "false" is that which has been shown to be untrue. Since the Enlightenment, the scientific rationale has not been to prove whether things are true, but whether they really occur. One of the principal difficulties in relation to recovered memories of childhood abuse is that it is not clear what should be investigated: the veracity of the alleged abuse, the veracity of the memories, or the process of the therapy. Nor is it clear how these questions could be investigated empirically while they remain the focus of both the criminal and the civil courts. Of all the questions, it would probably be of most benefit to study the phenomenon of recovered memories in more detail in terms of both the context in which they occur, the nature of the therapeutic process involved (if applicable), and the attitude and stance of the therapist. The "falsehood" or otherwise of any such memories should be left to the courts, and experts should be reluctant to give evidence for either side without advising the court of the current lack of scientific evidence in this area.

The debate about "false" memories raises the issue of the nature and scope of the professional duties of mental health care professionals, and the dangers of stepping outside their expertise in pursuit of "justice". Few health care professionals have training in crime investigation, or of truth detection. What health care professionals can bring to situations where child abuse is suspected is a compassionate scepticism and a rigorous intellectual approach to enquiry. If doctors step out of their professional role (especially while maintaining that they have not done so), then they are unlikely to be of help to the people who are most distressed—both those who claim to have been abused, and their families who deny that such abuse took place. It is also unlikely that any good will come of professionals taking up polarized positions, especially when there is little empirical evidence to support the most extreme views.

CHAPTER TWO

"Children are liars aren't they?"— an exploration of denial processes in child abuse

Arnon Bentovim

In this chapter, Arnon Bentovim looks at social denial, denial and the court system, denial concerning abuse of very young children, and denial in perpetrators. He provides a clinical and research overview.

At a recent meeting, a distinguished barrister repeated in conversation the often heard remark—"Children are liars aren't they?" This was said forcefully, with a sense of anger and blame. Our response was a retort, with equal vehemence, that adults were far more competent and skilful liars than children ever could be. The barrister's response was to state that the effect of children's lies could be absolutely devastating to those against whom untruths were levelled. Male teachers had lost their jobs and lives had been ruined as a result. Although we felt inclined to say that adults' lies had led to the destruction of civilizations, we hesitated to enter the dialectic.

Instead, we said that perhaps it was a question of who was assessing the child's statement in terms of judging whether statements were true or false. This led into an interesting discussion about the problems of current approaches to police investigation. Because it is now accepted that children do speak the truth, in an allegation of abuse this leads to a serious investigation. To investigate a complaint without interference requires that, for example, a teacher or a residential worker has to be suspended, a parent has to be asked to leave the home, or a child has to be removed from a home. The process in itself, it could be argued, could set in train extremely destructive consequences, and what was required was a different approach to the assessment, more open and balanced.

In broadening the discussion, we put forward the view that in France the Children's Judge, with his or her team of workers, undertook the investigation of statements made by children, and this could lead to a more balanced approach. The barrister's response was to say that the problem with the French system was that such officials have absolute power and did not necessarily have the training and experience to use such power wisely. He felt that the Scottish system was preferable where the Procurator Fiscal, a legally trained experienced official, took charge of the assessment and ensured that proper weight was given to statements, and investigations were carried out in a way that properly protected all involved, maintaining an open mind.

Children's statements

The comfortable reality that children were liars held sway until child protection professionals and feminist activists showed that children did experience serious sexual abuse of a long-standing nature and that denial and disavowal of responsibility was the norm rather than an exception.

Research has shown that children do have accurate memory of early events, that traumatic effects can register whether in memory or action from the first two years of life (Gaensbauer & Siegel, 1995).

The issue of adult denial

However, no matter how accurate our assessments and skilful our putting together the jigsaw-puzzle pieces of abuse, there will always be the problem of denial of their actions by adults who perpetrate, and disbelief in their families that abuse can have occurred. In our study of a series of 98 children diagnosed as having been sexually abused (Hyde et al., 1997), only 9% of adult or adolescent abusers took full responsibility for their abusive action whether there had been prosecution or care proceedings or not. A further 16% took a degree of responsibility for what was alleged, but 75% took no responsibility and denied that abuse had occurred. Similarly, 37% of the partners of the abuser could not agree or accept that abuse had occurred. This meant that at the end of a period of follow up where treatment was offered to all family members who were accepting that abuse had occurred, less than 10% of the children could be rehabilitated both to their abuser and their caring parent. Around 30% were still living in alternative care contexts—for example, children's homes, foster-care, therapeutic communities. Sixty per cent of the abused children were living with a family member, usually the care-taking parent.

This is an indication of how pervasive is the original denial response to the diagnosis of abuse. Once denial processes have been initiated, they continue to a very considerable degree. There were exceptions and there were adults who subsequently did take responsibility for abusive action, and caring parents who could acknowledge that abuse must have occurred, but these were the exceptions rather than the rule. We could be accused of having misdiagnosed sexual abuse and of being convinced by statements that had been planted. However, the majority of cases were tested in court—civil or criminal—and we excluded cases that on review were doubtful.

Understanding the denial process

How can we make sense of denial that occurs to such an extent that it means children have to be separated from their parents long-term, that offender treatment programmes which are increasing in their numbers and effectiveness are rejected by a significant number of parents, and that disruption of care, discontinuity, rejection, and distress is perpetuated for children through maternal disbelief? Research on the longer-term effects indicated that although children were often relieved at being out of their families and that abuse had stopped, there was intense grief and distress at the loss of the only families they knew. The mental health of children who were disbelieved was more negatively affected than those who were believed, and a significant number of rejected children and young people show considerable symptoms of depression and anxiety at follow-up despite having been involved in what was a successful treatment programme for other children who were protected, supported, and believed. Although penetrative abuse (Mannerino, Cohen, Smith, & Moore-Mutily, 1992; Mullen, Romans, Walton, & Herbison, 1988) has been shown to have serious longer-term "sleeper" effects, it is our view that the pernicious affect of disbelief, disavowal, and rejection is profound and affects personality functioning in the years following.

Psychological denial

Trepper and Barrett (1989) have described denial pragmatically as either *psychological denial* or *social denial*. By psychological denial, they imply that there is a process that could be described as repression. There appears to be a true absence of any conscious memory of having abused, even when the evidence of such action is strong. The absence of memory can only be established through the subjective report of the alleged perpetrator. However, we reported a case in 1991 that seemed to be a true case of psychological denial.

A stepfather had been imprisoned for abuse of his stepchildren. He hoped to re-establish contact with them and also with the children's mother, who had rejected him because of her belief in her children's statement. We accepted his demand for hypnotic regression, and he proved a good subject and within two or three sessions was beginning to regress in time to the period when he was living with the children and their mother. He began to express extremely severe depressive and self-destructive feelings as he got closer to the point when allegations were made against him. We stopped the process of hypnotic regression as being too much of a threat to his own life. The children had no wish to see him.

When assessing individuals who are denying any abusive action, we ask what their response would be if, for instance, they woke up one morning and became aware of memories of having carried out the sort of actions that a child had alleged against them. Alternatively, we might ask: if there was a grain in truth in what the child had stated, how would they feel? The immediate response is frequently that the man could not live with himself, would "top himself", commit suicide, it would be intolerable. It is not possible to distinguish whether this is the response of someone who has literally deleted memories, or whether it is a form of social denial. There is a near-universal awareness that such actions are socially intolerable and will lead to shame, ignominy, and universal abhorrence, so that denial is the automatic initial response whatever the later response—persisting denial or grudging acceptance.

One mechanism for the absence of memory on the perpetrator's part may be the avoidant response associated with experiencing an overwhelming traumatic event. It may well be that, although the abuser has been subject to overwhelming impulses to act, committing the act may have a traumatizing effect on the abuser.

A father who had shaken his infant so severely as to cause blindness and subdural haematoma denied the process for many months after. He had initially held one of his partner's children responsible and had only begun to acknowledge some responsibility after a period of therapeutic work. He grasped a doll when we asked him what had happened, and he described his mounting frustration at his inability to stop the baby crying when in his care. He described the fact that he was literally able to pilot a fifty-ton tank around narrow lanes but the care of this infant totally defeated him. He felt absolutely powerless and overwhelmed with rage at her crying. He talked about something snapping and of shaking the baby to stop the cries. Then he described something snapping in him. He felt overwhelmed at what he had done, and his action appeared to have traumatized him. This led to the second snap, possibly associated with an avoidant response.

Young people who lose control and hurt other children describe the way that the image of the hurt child haunts them in the form of flashbacks and disturbs their sleep with nightmares and re-enactments of the effect of their own actions. There is thus reason to believe that an abuser may be traumatized by his actions, and the avoidant response may lead to a deletion of thought and a blotting out of the event.

Social denial

Social denial occurs when there is a degree of awareness that there is responsibility for abusive action, but there is a process of denial, minimization, blaming others, or trivializing the situation. The perpetrator who is in a psychological state of denial/serious avoidance will protest his innocence vigorously, will blame the child for being a liar, will blame the professional for implanting ideas in the child's mind. The individual accused of abuse who is not in fact responsible will inevitably have the same responses, whilst the individual socially denying to avoid what he perceives as the consequences of his action will also make similar statements. Professionals and others can, of course, be recruited by such forceful statements, and the voice of the adult is inevitably going to be louder and more persuasive than a child who is in the grip of traumatic processes and is inevitably tentative, unsure, and confused about his or her reality (Summit, 1983).

Social denial can take the form of acknowledging that sexual abuse has occurred but somebody else is blamed as the perpetrator. A forceful statement is made that the child has a grievance against the alleged perpetrator, and therefore he is being blamed for something he did not do. Another variation is to state that although some contact may have occurred, the child must be mistaken about the adult's intention and there was only ordinary contact and affection and no abusive action. There may be a partial acceptance of responsibility for some actions which may be more acceptable and with others being denied; for example, a statement made by a 15-year-old may indicate that, after a gradual development of abusive contact (e.g. fondling and vaginal intercourse), anal rape may then have occurred. When the perpetrator is shown the statement or the video of what is alleged against him, he may accept that there was contact and maybe even attempted vaginal intercourse, but deny anal rape. The girl's mother, when shown the same statement, may only accept that there was contact with the breasts and fondling and refute any possibility that there could have been vaginal or anal intercourse. Subsequently, the child herself may create a different reality that it had not happened at all—22% of children withdrew their statements under such pressure.

Abuse occurring when perpetrators are drunk is another context for social denial: for example, "Well if she said I did this it must be the case, but I was drunk so I'm not truly responsible."

Denial and the court system

Because the English system in particular is adversarial, the issues of reliability and validity of children's statements—whether in the criminal or care system—are tested to a very high level. Despite the use of the video link or videos, the child has to be submitted to cross-questioning, and the search for inconsistency of statements becomes the test of validity. The perpetrator may be on trial, or the parents at risk of losing care of a child, but it is the children's evidence or the evidence emerging during assessment interviews that comes under the most careful and detailed scrutiny.

In the criminal court, unlike the civil court, expert witnesses cannot be called to help a jury understand the process by which children's experiences may be deleted from awareness, or details elaborated as a result of the effect of post-traumatic states on the perceptions and reality of a child's experience. Thus, the court has no way of being assisted to assess the statements made by children in the criminal court context.

In the care context, the adversarial process ensures that there will be intense scrutiny and criticism of professionals' interviewing techniques. Thus it is hoped that the judge can be convinced that the test to show that a child has been abused by a particular perpetrator cannot be met on a balance of probabilities. There is less scrutiny of the statements made by abusers, and even the recourse to lie-detectors or penile plethysmographs is unsatisfactory, as these can all be falsified by a determined perpetrator. The Faithful Foundation (lecture given by Wyre and Eldridge in 1995) carried out extended two-day interviews with perpetrators and attempted to assess whether their thinking and general attitudes to children may be consistent with what is known of the pattern of thinking of abusers who do take responsibility for abuse. This approach—which pays as much attention to the detailed way in which abusers present themselves as to the detailed assessment of the victims—is clearly a necessary approach in the service of natural justice.

Trauma-organized systems
as an exploratory model for denial processes

An approach to understanding the range of denial processes is the application of a trauma-organized system theory. Bentovim (1992) put forward a view that trauma-organized systems can be considered a key theory to the understanding of physical and sexual abuse in families. The frame is a sociocultural one in the sense that society is seen as a context in which women and children are looked at both as requiring protection yet also as appropriate objects for violence. Thus, the family as the agent of culture is an organization that can protect, nurture, and facilitate children's development and growth, but it can also be an organization that inhibits, abuses, and constrains the development of children growing within it.

It is our view that the way that traumatic events are processed by individuals, by families, and in society in general comes to organize thinking and narratives. Traumatic events are, by definition, stressful events that overwhelm defensive capacities. Through intense affective arousal associated with helplessness and intense distress, they may even come to be represented in the brain in a different way to less affect-laden memories and evoke a particular set of responses. These are well delineated in the increasingly differentiated notion of traumatic and post-traumatic stress. They take the form of re-enactment, flashbacks, nightmares, and triggering of distressing memories of the abuse, which systemically alternate with struggles to avoid thinking and feeling resulting in dissociative avoidant states and considerable restriction of individual functioning. Such responses also trigger the intense pattern of arousal, fear, fright, and disruption of sleep. This state is described as having an adaptive function in terms of preparation for future self-protective actions. They can come to overwhelm and organize the psychological life of that individual, particularly as, in child abuse, experiences are likely to be repeated.

Recent research on factors that lead to an abusive orientation in young people indicates that a pervasive history of experiencing physical violence directly, or witnessing physical violence in the family, has a profound effect on relationship style and the development of an abusive orientation. Even beyond the sexual abuse itself, such an orientation has a profound organizing effect on the wish to divest the self of victimization by finding somebody else to be hurt instead, the motive may be to seek revenge and to ensure that the other shall not feel free of the oppression by which the perpetrating individual feels persecuted.

This process affects choice of partner, either through interlocking pathology or targeting, leading to the development of which is a family system focused on adult needs with children having to comply. An aspect of the child is perceived as being defiant or sexually inviting, justifying adult punitive responses or sexual action. The caring parent—who may herself have been abused and is therefore in a dissociated state—may be undermined and disqualified and therefore unable to perceive the child's distress. A family story grows that defines the child as deserving punishment, or as promiscuous or bad, leading to rejection and poor care. A child in such a situation will reveal the abuse in the way described by Summit (1983) in the Accommodation Syndrome: partial, tentative, and inviting disqualification. The attribution of self-blame, compounded with threats and bullying, leads the child to retract and deny his or her experiences under pressure. When allegations are made, the abuser, fearing retaliation and persecution, is driven to organize professionals or families, through intimidation and threat, to reinforce psychological or social denial. Thus the trauma-organized system, which justifies abuse, is transformed into a denial process of the reality and continues the process of disqualification and treating the child as a thing. It is alleged that those who support the child are mistaken and are leading the child on, rather than being considered as helping the child to externalize the narrative and share the traumatic experience.

An example of the narratives or conversations that reflect these trauma-organizing processes is that of a 13-year-old girl separated from her family after allegations of abuse against her stepfather. Although she gave an account with richness of detail embedded in a context that seemed believable and was also backed up by medical evidence, in the criminal court she was unable to make a statement even using the video link. The stepfather was a large, intimidating, and frightening figure, and she felt quite unable to speak even though she was in different part of the court speaking through a video link. The criminal case therefore had to be dropped, and the father's response was that this proved that he was indeed innocent. The case was then taken up in the civil court, and the 4-year-old son of the stepfather and the mother was also part of the proceedings as it was felt that he, too, was at risk, given the abusive actions described against the stepdaughter. As we explored with the mother the statements that her daughter had made, we asked her whether she thought that her daughter was basically a liar—was she the sort of girl who habitually told stories that subsequently turned out to be false?

The mother's immediate response was to say that no, she was not, at which point her husband turned to her and said forcefully: "Don't you remember that you have said that you wouldn't believe that I was capable of doing such a thing to your daughter unless you saw it with your eyes." The mother acceded to this statement, and the conversation ceased. The man then forcefully put his point over that, if the court had not found him guilty, there was no case to answer, and why should the civil court not accept the criminal court's views. We then noted that the 4-year-old was mimicking his father's way of speech, banging on the table, making guttural growling noises. Thus the abrasive, forceful, silencing, oppressive style of conversation is maintained, silencing and negating reality. It is not surprising that children from such family contexts elaborate the avoidant response and can become extremely resistant to attempts to help them process their experiences and can adopt a self-denying, self-punitive, and self-destructive stance. We also note that, when children can be supported to the point where they are prepared to give evidence, a significant proportion of abusers do then plead guilty.

* * *

In another family, a father who had had several years of therapeutic work was able to tell his family how he had literally oppressed and controlled them during the period when he was abusing their daughter. The father pleaded guilty, rather than put his daughter through the process of having to give evidence against him. He did not employ another form of social denial—which is to say that a parent would not wish his child to suffer the humiliation of giving evidence against him and therefore he would plead guilty; the next statement to be made in these circumstances is, of course, that the abuse did not occur!

* * *

A final example of this process is that of a 15-year-old who had been literally raped by her stepfather. The abuse had come to light because she had such a serious bleeding episode that she had to be rushed to hospital to receive treatment. During the waiting phase before the criminal hearing whilst on bail, the judge gave permission for him to be able to spend time in the family home, provided that he slept at his mother's house. Although the Social Services department were most concerned about the implications of this, the mother and the child involved were adamant that they wanted him to spend time at home in this way. We carried out an assessment of therapeutic needs, and the girl adamantly refused to come for any group

work, saying that she had no symptoms, was not upset by what
had happened, and did not wish to have any help. We asked
her how she coped with the fact that she was seeing so much of
her stepfather. We asked her whether seeing him reminded her
of her abuse—did she not have flashbacks, distressing memories, as so many other girls told us? She said, no, she did not,
because she had constructed a different picture in her mind.
She told herself that it was not her stepfather who had raped
her, but somebody who had broken into their house, an in-
truder, who had carried out the rape. In addition, there was
concern that her stepfather was suffering from serious agora-
phobia and could not leave the home in any case. Therapeutic
work was impossible here, and the trauma-organized system
had literally frozen matters into a process of avoidance and
created a reality that negated traumatic actions and responses.
This is an example of an avoidant trauma-organized system.

Denial in the abuse of younger children

Many of the cases that we have discussed so far have involved
older children. The children's statements are often elaborate or
convincing, and there may be medical evidence, yet even so there
are high levels of denial and disbelief. The situation can be even
more extreme with young children, who are less clear in their
statements, are more easily silenced, and are more prone to elaborate or negate and find it far more difficult to provide detail that is
convincing. The level of abhorrence and disgust at those abusing
very young children is so high that the cost of taking responsibility
is also seen to be much higher, and the recruitment of other family
members or professionals to negate the possibility is at an even
higher level. It could be argued that much of the storm around
the Cleveland Inquiry arose because the diagnosis of sexual abuse
being made involved very much younger children. The level of
disgust at the idea of anal abuse of very young children was so
high that it fuelled disbelief. A system rapidly became organized
to blame the paediatricians rather than accept the possibility of
abuse. The finding in later years that a considerable proportion of
the children had indeed been abused cast a different light on the

whole process of outrage, which was the predominant emotion at the time.

A group of highly experienced professionals were gathered to see whether they could reach agreement in their views. A subsequent Consensus Statement (Lamb, 1995) was produced which expressed the view that although young children can be helped, using skilful interviewing, to describe their experiences in ways that are convincing, the evidence is that many younger children tend to resist attempts to help them speak. Ceci and Bruck (1993), in their historical review and synthesis, also point out that even very young children are capable of recalling much that is forensically relevant; they also point out their vulnerability to post-event suggestions. There is also evidence, however, of a refusal to speak about known events.

Saywitz, Goodman, Nicholas, and Moan (1991) asked 5- and 7-year-old children who attended for genital or anal examinations, versus examinations for scoliosis, about their experience. Only 22% of children reported genital touching and 11% anal touching, compared to all children mentioning their backs being examined in the scoliosis clinic. Presumably, young children find it difficult to talk about their private parts.

There are four studies where sexual abuse is substantiated by means other than statements. Sorenson and Snow (1991) noted 72% of children denying sexual abuse initially, and 22% recanting after disclosure; only 11% actively disclosed without tentative features. Faller (1988) and Terri (1991) reported similar results. Lawson and Chaffin (1992) reviewed the records of children diagnosed as having venereal disease and later interviewed to assess sexual abuse; 57% failed to reveal the source of infection, and 83% of children whose parents were unsupportive of possible sexual abuse did not tell.

Conclusion

Extreme difficulty at dealing with allegations (or suspicions in the case of younger children) of sexual abuse indicates that it may be essential to find new ways of dealing with denial and avoidant responses in people with an abusive orientation towards younger children. Despite the use of video evidence via a video link, the difficulties in bringing successful prosecutions where young children are involved are very considerable, and the number of cases considered suitable to prosecute is small. The fact that there is no way of diverting prosecution processes, or finding alternatives to the judicial process, means that social denial as the predominant response will continue. Civil proceedings are demanding higher and higher levels of proof, so that this also leads to a risk of children being unprotected.

Although denial processes are so powerful, the rate of actual prosecution and conviction for sexual abuse has increased very markedly in recent years. There is an increasing provision of treatment for offenders both within the prison service and outside, yet despite the growth in understanding of abusive processes, the response to conviction remains predominantly one of imprisonment rather than of probation orders together with treatment. The cost for the offender of taking responsibility is therefore a high one, and the advantage of denial may often seem to outweigh the benefits to the child and family. Thus, despite evidence to the contrary, children will go on being called liars!

CHAPTER THREE

Trauma, skin: memory, speech

Ann Scott

> *In this chapter, Ann Scott looks at the role of language and speech in the false memory debate. Drawing on the psychoanalytic work of Henri Rey, she provides a careful linguistic analysis of the pain involved in this subject.*

O ne of the first features to strike us when we consider the question of false memory and the controversy that it has generated is the role of speech both in organizing the terms of the debate and in preserving the anguish for those involved, in both generations of the families. I use a word as strong as anguish deliberately: the briefest survey of the ephemera of the False Memory Syndrome Foundation shows how much pain is embedded in the letters and statements of those who feel themselves to be falsely accused (see, for example, FMS, 1993; for the FMSF's Affiliated Group in Britain, see ACAP, 1993). Because it is increasingly recognized that sexual abuse is a profound impingement of boundaries, psychic and actual, we tend to react with anger to a "denial of the truth" on the part of a parent accused of abuse (who is most likely, of course, to be the father). But I want to suggest that it is in the nature of this situation as a whole—where memories are so much at odds—that words can, to cite Henri Rey (1986), "be expelled as unwanted objects" (p. 185), by both daughters and parents. Furthermore, since sexual abuse and the memories associated with it concern the body, I want to suggest that it is through considering something about the relationship, felt and linguistic, between words and the subjective sense of the skin as the body's boundary that we might be able to account for at least some of the uncontained feel that this debate has come to have and the experience of puzzlement that many have at the irreconcilably different accounts of the family members involved. My text is the reported speech of concerned journalism, and I am examining the issue through the lens of an idea about dialogue evolved within the clinical setting.

Let us assume, first of all, that the memory of a trauma can be recovered—as the British Psychological Society's survey data suggest (Morton et al., 1995)—then what strikes us in the situation is how *violent* the debate around false memory syndrome has become. Here it may be important to note that whether or not sexual abuse is known to have taken place—indeed, whether or not it may have taken place, is being denied by the accused parent (who knows consciously he committed the acts) or is being denied by the accused parent (who is genuinely in denial), has been remembered all along by the daughter, or had been unknown and then remembered in adult life—a cultural taboo is being violated at the level of language, if not at the level of the body. For one of the paradoxes about the discourse of incest at the moment is that even though transgressions of the incest taboo are now increasingly accepted as widespread in practice, the taboo as a cultural requirement continues to exercise its demands. So, something unthinkable is seen to have been thought; and, because it is seen as the unthinkable, its expression in words is met with aggression.

Beatrix Campbell demonstrates beautifully, to my mind, how this process shows itself in the culture, in her fine account of three cases where abuse was denied (Campbell, 1995). Although her purpose is to subvert the false memory argument by showing that in these particular cases the abuse had been spoken of by the young women before they had had any therapy—so that what was in play was not recovered or false memory at all—her article illustrates very well the level of hostility, fear, disruption, and disturbance that such words and memories are bound still to elicit. The language is, strikingly, one of warfare as mediated by the journalist's voice. Let me quote just one of her vignettes: a daughter and her mother, in

> a middle-class family whose usual unhappiness has been detonated by a young woman in her twenties whose way of living with herself is self-destruction, starvation and attempted suicide. The daughter has always known why she was trying to die. When she tells her story her body buckles, her voice fades and the blood drains from her taut face. Despite her difficulty, and despite her mother's disbelief, her narrative is crisp and eloquent. [p. 27]

The wife insisted that her husband and her father could not have abused her daughter:

> She rages, she weeps, she harangues her daughter's hospital, she has become a procedural vigilante, she keeps voluminous files of correspondence with the health and social services. She claims her daughter got her ideas from books, from other patients, from dreams, but not from her own experience. She fires False Memory Syndrome literature at the young woman. Their conversations are consumed by it. [p. 28]

Both these women's words are unwanted by those to whom they are addressed. Because the experience is contested—as the title of this book, *Memory in Dispute*, reminds us—those involved are left with unusually raw, unheard words and the impassioned reactions that they evoke, as are we, the readers. How might we think about such angry sequences? Very speculatively, I want to suggest that Henri Rey's work on psycholinguistic structures (Rey, 1986) may offer a helpful starting point for at least some of the exchanges that are in play. I do not overlook the difference of setting, and it could be argued that the two registers—clinical and journalistic—are too different to be discussed in this way. On the other hand, the media's concern with false memory syndrome (an extension of its concern with sexual abuse generally) has been on a scale that invites deeper consideration and may be helped, I am suggesting, by ideas evolved within the clinical setting.

Rey's general argument is that sounds normally become words through projective identification, and that words can be seen as objects: the argument builds up slowly, and I can only quote selectively from it:

> [T]he sound-word—the sound becoming a word as it acquires domain (meaning)—is at the same time acquiring an inside space, like we have seen for other objects. This *inside of words, or words as containers*, is brought to our attention through a great number of expressions in the language. . . . Phenomena of displacement and condensation, achieved by projective and introjective identification, structure objects. Words are similarly structured. Experiences are projected into sounds, making them words by projective identification. Thus when words are used, *they evoke the experiences they contain*. [Rey, 1986, p. 184; emphasis added]

The suggestion, then, is for words to be seen as "structured like any other objects" (p. 183), and as being "used for the interiorization of experiences or structures, and the fixation of these experiences in memory" (p. 185). These ideas can act as a marker, in my view, in making sense of the quality of the disputes around false or recovered memory. For here it is an *un*certainty or elusiveness of experience, terrifying for those involved, which permeates everything: words, memory, violation of bodily and psychic space—all seem to have become rootless, mobile; the words seem to lack an inside space, at least as they are reported by the journalist.

We might also speculate that this "inside space of words" is normally paralleled—or even made possible—by the sense of inside space that is created by the skin as boundary between inside and outside. Where abuse has taken place, or is *felt* by the subject to have taken place, the sense of disturbance in the continuity of the skin as a boundary may make words less stably present for him or her. In the special case where memory is beginning to emerge in adulthood, the words have no history of being bound to an experience of which the subject is confident. So, what is likely to happen when an adult daughter is faced with the dilemma of attempting to communicate, within her family, what she now, however tentatively, believes is a memory of something actual that happened—which at the same time would represent the violation of a taboo that is part of the cultural and linguistic context in which all are placed? My suggestion is that her words become "unwanted objects", and in that process their volatility is assured.

To amplify: Rey attempts first, as I have mentioned, to map the nature not of this type of highly charged communication in particular, but of the relationship in principle between speaker and listener in any exchange. Taking up René Thom's work, Rey focuses particularly on the concept of "semantic density", which, broadly, grades words according to their volatility when they are spoken (Rey, 1986, p. 181). The account of the semantic density of different parts of speech is somewhat technical but could, I think, be imaginatively invoked in situations of newly remembered abuse to make sense of a phenomenon that is a puzzling feature of some (but not all) recovered memory narratives: the susceptibility to retraction, the evaporation of conviction when daughters take back their accusations. I should stress that here I am concerned only with those cases where the impasse across the generations is maintained; not where daughters have, over time, come to believe their memories were not reliable and a reconciliation has been achieved.

On the face of it an overly chemical term, the notion of "evaporation" may shed light on the paradoxical disparity seen in some of the cases: between a sufferer's continuing symptoms and the change that her speech may undergo. Take the charge "You abused me" or "My father abused me", later retracted—what is at work when such a conviction is given up? (My stress is on the exchanges reported in the many media accounts, not on the clinical exchanges in which the "You" may refer, in the transference, to the analyst.) According to Rey, here focusing on the elements of speech themselves, a verb will in principle be more "volatile" than a substantive, and, in a transitive sentence, the object will be more volatile, less semantically dense than the subject—that is, certain words will disappear, others remain in place. Could the concept of semantic density help us to map the volatility of the communication we often see in media accounts of false or recovered memory dynamics? I am suggesting that if the words are not held by their recipient (and it is not surprising that they are not), they function as "unwanted objects" and are less likely to remain stable for the one who speaks them.

In these dynamics it is painfully clear that resonance between speaker and recipient is lacking; there is no linguistic communication. In the sentence "You abused me", for example, the verb would be the most volatile, then the object, while the subject— here, the father—would crucially remain in place. Again, the other's "flat denial" might lead to an evaporation into thin air of the most volatile elements of the subject's memory, leaving the speaker utterly bereft of confirmation and vulnerable to retraction. The troubling ending that Campbell (1995) leaves us, her readers, with highlights the point. Why has the young woman whose abuse was denied gone on to make another suicide attempt? Could it be born of a fantasy? Who put the memories into her head? "Nobody did but me", she says in her retraction (p. 28). The reader is understandably disturbed by the apparent *volte face*. But as Campbell writes—tellingly, to my mind—"the syntax if not the substance of her story" had changed (p. 28).

This is not to say, on the other hand, that the resolution of the daughter's pain would depend only on her father ultimately affirming her experience. That would be to ignore the psychic processes at work in him, and also to assume that reliability of memory is itself a straightforward matter. Indeed, it may be a mistake to treat the issues raised by the false memory controversy as though they were of a different order altogether from those raised by sexual abuse that has always been remembered. In individual cases, of course, the situations will be different: since it is increasingly accepted that sexual abuse can be damaging at many levels, one might expect more uncertainty about the effects in cases where memories begin to emerge in adult life but in fact remain very shadowy. Symptoms may be more nebulous. From another angle, however, a clear distinction between "actual" and "imagined" may also be becoming harder to maintain. Parental behaviour that may have been intrusive, though falling short of actual abuse, may appear as memories that have metaphorical rather than literal truth (Phil Mollon, quoted in Grant, 1995; see also chapter 10, this volume). Also, as Lesley Stubbings, who sued for compensation after memory of her abuse returned in adulthood, said in a television interview: "When you're a child you haven't got a vocabulary. You don't think 'I've been violated'"(First Sight, 1995).

At source, sexual abuse—whether real or imagined, always known, or reconstructed in adulthood—involves the skin and feelings about the skin and its sensations early in life, for before there is adult speech there is the bodily experience—actual, imagined, or metaphorical. Here is Linda, an adult woman in a sensitive television documentary, recalling early sexual abuse, remembered as an adult; she is shot in close-up and framed so that her eyes are not visible, and we see only her nose, mouth, and chin. The aggressive editing of the image enhances the effect of her words:

> This thing in my mouth . . . a shape . . . I started getting this choking feeling—and somehow I knew it was a penis . . . a razor blade close to my chest. [First Sight, 1995]

These are not the benign, nurturant skin sensations that Esther Bick described as giving evidence of a containing object—the joining of nipple and mouth (see Bick, 1986; Hinshelwood, 1991a, 1991b)—but the malign, confusing skin contact that disrupts peace and safety. Here we could say that the father's skin has failed to be the skin that the infant-child needs. Again, very speculatively, we might take Bick's picture of the object that fails to contain (and, by extension, the internal containing object that fails to contain) as being felt as a partial skin, as tending to develop holes, and link it, forwards in time, with the daughter's psychic predicament. Here her own skin feels "partial" and her words have come to lack their inside space. I am suggesting that the skin contact of father and daughter has had its primitive traumatic effect.

In some cases, of course, the sense of the early experience will only be recovered in adult life; where this is then denied by the parents, the adult daughter is faced with a psychic gap, a further lack of containment: the original trauma is compounded by the trauma of a denial. The daughter's words, which lack their inside space because of disturbance in the boundary of the body, lack stability. Her situation is, I am suggesting, reminiscent of that of the infant where the primitive skin contact has "leaked". Bick, to quote Eric Rhode (1994),

concentrates on aspects of infancy in which there is a falling-
apart or a leaking of a provisional holding-together. The
infants exist as actions in a nowhere that is everywhere. . . .
Their feelings derive from sensations: they have little sense of
internal *figures* to whom they might relate. [p. 270]

To extend this point, one might suggest that the words go into
or come from a kind of limitless space. As one mother said, ""I
don't know where these false memories are founded", and yet she
is certain that "these amazing allegations came out in therapy"
(quoted in Campbell, 1995, p. 27). With this we are brought back to
the virulence that is in play. I come to a final point: that the sense of
danger is felt not just by those who are accused. As Rey says,
words can be felt as "dangerous objects inside" as well (1986, p.
184), so the accuser feels guilty about the accusation too. And just
as Rey describes a patient who simulated suicide many times in
order to have her stomach washed out, "because she said that
words were mouldy, poisonous, dangerous objects inside her
stomach, and if she talked they would hit the therapist and do him
great harm" (p. 184), so memory may not always be benign—far
from it. Campbell describes an incident in which one young
woman saw something in a Christmas catalogue which reminded
her of her baby brother being abused with a toy. "It was a memory
she hated having", she says baldly and movingly (1995, p. 28).

I have been suggesting that the "trauma of false memory" is a
crisis at the level of speech as well as a crisis at the level of the
body. Let me end, by way of contrast, with an example from the
more crafted language of poetry. Emily Dickinson's lines "The
Body—borrows a Revolver—/He bolts the Door", from her poem
"One need not be a Chamber—to be Haunted—" (1863, p. 333) also
indicate how powerfully productive, and yet violent, words can be
in representing sensations at the level of the body. We can recognize, however, that despite the sense of exposure—and danger—in
the words chosen, the addressee is in no sense implicated as accused. By contrast, the speech of the adult daughter who recovers
memory has gone further and is sometimes (and understandably)
accusatory. Yet it is a form of speech which in the nature of things
may act as an "unwanted object" to its recipient and, because of
that, circulate in an uncontained space. Interestingly, as we know,

some of those who have recovered memories have not sought to confront their abusers or, ultimately, take legal action. They have intuitively preferred to allow the memories to stay inside. And if they *are* able to maintain the sense of an "inside space" that is safe, their healing may perhaps prove more stable.

Acknowledgements

I am very grateful to Valerie Sinason, Lesley Caldwell, Bob Hinshelwood, Meira Likierman, Marilyn Pietroni, and Jean Radford for their help and comments on a first draft of this chapter; and to an informal seminar around the paper in September 1996, organized by Prophecy Coles.

CHAPTER FOUR

The psychoanalytic concept of repression: historical and empirical perspectives

Brett Kahr

In this historical chapter, Brett Kahr takes us through the history of the term "repression" and Freud's views on memory and "primal repression" and "repression proper". He also examines contemporary attempts to prove the existence of repression in psychological tests.

"All repressions are of *memories.*"

Sigmund Freud (1910, p. 31).

A case of forgetting

On 8 January 1908, a little boy from Vienna called Herbert Graf, aged 4¾ years, visited the zoological collection at the Austrian imperial palace at Schönbrunn, accompanied by his mother, Olga Graf. This particular excursion proved somewhat traumatic, and, as the day progressed, little Herbert began to develop a marked phobia of horses. He not only became fearful of stepping outdoors, but also fretted that a horse might bite him. The boy's father, Max Graf, a distinguished musicologist, took his son for a consultation with Professor Sigmund Freud, who encouraged Herr Graf to treat the young child according to the new insights of psychoanalysis. Freud himself supervised this pioneering venture in child analysis, and within a matter of months, Herbert's symptoms abated considerably. Eventually, Freud (1909b) published the details of the case, changing the name of the patient from little Herbert to the immortal "Little Hans".

Some fourteen years later, in the spring of 1922, Herbert Graf, now a robust lad of 19, visited Freud. He told the professor that although he eventually came to read the monograph that Freud wrote about him, "the whole of it came to him as something un-known; he did not recognize himself; he could remember nothing" (Freud, 1922c, p. 148). Somehow, Herbert Graf seems to have obliterated an enormous amount of life experience from his conscious mind. Although Graf's father had recorded a great deal of his son's actual childhood speech in painstaking detail, Herbert Graf could remember none of it directly, even after he had read Freud's case history, which might perhaps have jogged his memory.

Freud's writings on repression

This brief vignette from the annals of psychoanalytic history serves as but one instance which illustrates the vagaries of human memory. For many centuries, the study of memory systems remained a matter of relatively small interest. Through the years, those investigators who have actually written about the subject have contributed some often outlandish tracts on memory functioning. For example, during antiquity, the philosopher Diogenes postulated that the act of forgetting results from a disruption in the appropriate distribution of air throughout the different parts of the body. Many years later, even René Descartes hypothesized that disturbances of memory might result from a failure of certain animal spirits to move successfully throughout the brain. By the late nineteenth century, the burgeoning discipline of experimental psychology provided scientists with new methods for studying memory in a systematic fashion. Large numbers of scholars, from

Hermann Ebbinghaus in the nineteenth century to Ulric Neisser in the twentieth century, have provided a set of theories that have guided an extensive body of empirical research. But even with Professor Neisser's concentration on the more practical applications of memory studies, the preoccupation with this work has remained, by and large, the province of relatively sequestered, academic behavioural scientists.

In recent years, the subject of human memory has become a focus of considerable interest in view of recent debates surrounding the so-called false memory syndrome. Journalists who have written on this controversy have implied that mental health professionals and research scholars have only recently begun to grapple with the problem of "true memory" and "false memory"—but let us pause to remember that Sigmund Freud had already devoted nearly half a century of sustained contemplation to this very topic. In view of Freud's considered writings on the topic of repressed memory, and in view of the growing body of empirical data which has arisen from Freud's theories, there may well be some merit in reviewing certain highlights from Freud's vast catalogue of observations on these matters.

The term "repression" entered the psychological literature at least as early as the first decades of the nineteenth century. The pundit Johann Friedrich Herbart [1776-1841] had already used the German term "Verdrängung" (repression) in his writings, and especially in his book of 1824, *Psychologie als Wissenschaft*, published several decades before Freud's birth. Freud himself first referred to repression in his article "On the Psychical Mechanism of Hysterical Phenomena: Preliminary Communication", written with Josef Breuer (Freud, 1893a). In reflecting on hysterical patients who had suffered from a psychical trauma, Breuer and Freud (1893a) spoke about "things which the patient wished to forget, and therefore intentionally repressed from his conscious thought" (p. 10). Freud (1927e, p. 153) would eventually come to refer to repression as the "oldest word in our psycho-analytic terminology".

In the early texts on the treatment of hysteria, Freud often used the terms "repression" and "defence" in an interchangeable fashion (cf. Freud, 1894a). Gradually, of course, Freud began to identify other specific mechanisms of defence such as conversion, isolation, projection, and so forth, and repression became only one of several

possible unconscious strategies for eliminating psychic pain from
the field of consciousness.

In his monograph on the life of Leonardo da Vinci, Freud made
a very important contribution to the study of childhood memories.
He wrote that: "Quite unlike conscious memories from the time of
maturity, they are not fixed at the moment of being experienced
and afterwards repeated, but are only elicited at a later age when
childhood is already past; in the process they are altered and falsified, and are put into the service of later trends, so that generally
speaking they cannot be sharply distinguished from phantasies"
(Freud, 1910c, p. 83). In this crucial passage, Freud has anticipated
virtually every one of the essential debating points in contemporary discussions over false memories, fully recognizing the sheer
complexity of teasing out true memories, and remarking that
childhood memories may readily become repressed, only to re-
emerge at a later point in the life cycle. In 1914, in his monograph
on the history of the psychoanalytic movement, Freud had actually
referred to repression, quite baldly, as "the corner-stone on which
the whole structure of psychoanalysis rests" (Freud, 1914d, p. 16),
ever aware of the vast extent of repressed memories.

By 1915, Sigmund Freud had observed innumerable instances
of repression in the course of his psychoanalytic work with
troubled patients, and he soon published a more clearly articulated theory of this subject in his article "Repression" (Freud,
1915d). This brief, but dense, text remains Freud's fullest statement
on the subject of repression, and, as such, it merits a fairly detailed
explication.

Freud began his essay by exploring the ways in which the
human organism attempts to protect itself from a painful or unbearable situation. He conceptualized repression primarily as a
flight from an intolerable idea that occurs in the mind. Freud noted
that if the unpleasant stimulus existed in external reality, such as
an attacking lion or tiger perhaps, then it would be natural to flee;
but when the stimulus thrives internally, then the organism must
flee from itself. Sadly, in such circumstances, "flight is of no avail,
for the ego cannot escape from itself" (Freud, 1915d, p. 146). Therefore, the ego must condemn a piece of psychic reality and utilize
the mechanism of repression to eradicate this psychic reality from
consciousness. Freud (1915d, p. 147) summarized this basic postu-

late in the following succinct manner: "*The essence of repression lies simply in turning something away, and keeping it at a distance, from the conscious.*" He also underscored that repression tends to be synonymous with the region of mental life known as the unconscious, which becomes the repository of banished or unbearable ideas and affects.

Freud further differentiated between two types of repression, called "primal repression" and "repression proper". Repression occurs in two phases. In the first phase, known as primal repression, the controversial piece of psychic life becomes obliterated from consciousness. In the second phase of repression, known as repression proper, all experiences intimately related to the repressed piece of psychic life undergo repression as well, so that the defence mechanism of repression infiltrates many areas of life. For example, if a young girl suffers from a traumatic rape by her father, and then blocks this memory from her mind, we would refer to this as primal repression. If then some years later this same young girl, now a woman, began to have sexual intercourse and found it distasteful, but did not know why, we would understand this as an expression of repression proper. In other words, all reincarnations of the original repressed event would themselves become subject to further repressions. In severe cases, abused children who then come to have sexual relations during adulthood may even repress the adult sexual activities entirely.

Thus, Freud has hypothesized that the effects of a single act of repression may continue unabated throughout the life cycle. He also indicated, however, that an instance of repression need not be total or comprehensive. Often, only an aspect of a certain event may be repressed; contemporary clinicians would refer to this as partial repression. Freud (1915d, p. 150) stressed that repression operates in "a *highly individual* manner" in all cases. Additionally, the utilization of repression will require a heightened cathexis of the libidinal energy: in other words, the emotional cost of repression will be extensive since we devote so much psychic energy to the maintenance of repressions. In crude terms, Freud has suggested that each of us has to work hard to remember that we must forget something.

Freud had observed that an act of repression results, sadly, in the formation of symptoms. He had already become aware of this finding in his work with Josef Breuer, described in the *Studies on Hysteria* (Freud, 1895d); but Freud had taken this opportunity to elaborate the theory further, based on the accumulation of additional clinical material. Freud (1918b[1914]) provided a clinical example from his work with the Russian aristocratic patient Sergéi Konstantínovich Pankéev, who developed an animal phobia. Freud commented that the patient did not really fear animals as such; rather, through the mechanism of repression and the further mechanism of displacement, Pankéev eliminated his fear of his own father and then came to locate the dangerous aspects of his father in the animals that he subsequently feared. This observation has had a profound impact upon the psychoanalytic treatment of anxiety states and phobic states, because Freud has suggested to us that whenever we express terror about a certain object, the psychoanalyst must actually help the patient to search for an earlier, more primitive object.

Sigmund Freud also realized that repressions could be lifted as a result of psychoanalytic treatment. In his essay "Mourning and Melancholia", Freud (1917e[1915], p. 256) commented that, "in analyses it often becomes evident that first one and then another memory is activated", and that after clinical treatment has progressed satisfactorily, repressed and unconscious memories can return to the fore of consciousness after lengthy periods of time. By 1926, Freud had published his complex book *Inhibitions, Symptoms and Anxiety*, in which he attempted to simplify his vocabulary of defence mechanisms somewhat by proposing that the term "defence" should be used for all forms of protecting the ego from dangerous intrusions, and that the term "repression" should be restricted specifically for cases of unconsciously motivated amnestic forgetting. He also noted that repression can result from anxiety.

The role of repression in the extensive writings of Sigmund Freud defies a brief summary. Peter Madison (1956, 1961) and Barbara Pendleton Jones (1993) have written worthy exegeses of the changing vicissitudes of Freud's concept of repression, and the interested scholar would do well to consult these sources for a more detailed treatment of the matter. For our purposes, we must underscore that although Freud often changed his theories throughout his lifetime, he never abandoned the concept of repression, and he insisted that his clinical data, derived from his work with highly distressed patients, urged him to continue his investigation into the way in which all human beings remove painful thoughts and feelings from consciousness.

Experimental research on repression

For more than fifty years, experimental psychologists have sought to investigate the validity of Freud's theories and psychotherapeutic techniques through the independent means of the psychological laboratory. The work of Matthew Hugh Erdelyi, an American research scientist, remains of particular relevance. In 1967, Ralph Norman Haber and Matthew Hugh Erdelyi, two cognitive psychologists, published a landmark article entitled "Emergence and Recovery of Initially Unavailable Perceptual Material", based upon a study conducted at Yale University. Both Haber and Erdelyi wanted to investigate whether the psychoanalytic procedure of free association would actually improve recall memory. According to psychoanalytic practitioners, the art of lying on the couch and free-associating facilitates the expression of hitherto repressed memories, and the subsequent unblocking of repressions thereby aids the recovery of the patient.

Haber and Erdelyi enlisted the cooperation of forty male undergraduate students from Yale University, who were shown a slide depicting a Southern scene containing a cotton-gin complex, complete with a loading platform, a suction pipe, a wagon, horses, workers, bales of cotton, various buildings, trees, and so forth. The subjects observed this picture for the swift duration of one hundred milliseconds, from a distance of fifteen feet (most people would barely be able to tell what they had seen consciously after having watched a certain stimulus picture for a mere one hundred milliseconds, or one tenth of a second). After being shown this brief stimulus, the subjects were then invited to draw on a piece of paper what they had only just seen. Thereafter, Haber and Erdelyi asked some of the subjects to begin free-associating, whereas other subjects had the opportunity to play a game of darts. Afterwards,

Haber and Erdelyi then asked all the students to draw the picture a second time.

Haber and Erdelyi discovered that those subjects who had the chance to free-associate in-between their first and second drawings revealed a great improvement in their memory of the original Southern scene stimulus, whereas by and large those who played darts did not improve. The experimenters concluded that the act of free-associating increases the ability to remember material outside of conscious awareness. Haber and Erdelyi scored the drawings for accuracy. After the first round of drawings, the free association sub-group scored 36.0 points on average, whereas the dart-throwing sub-group scored 38.5 points on average. After the free association, the average score in the free-association sub-group increased from 36.0 to 51.8, whereas the average score in the dart-throwing sub-group actually decreased from 38.5 to 32.0, thus suggesting a slight memory decay. The leap from 36.0 points to 51.8 points in the free association sub-group represents a highly statistically significant change. As a result of this work, the authors concluded: "The present study has experimentally demonstrated that genuine recoveries of below-conscious material can and in fact do occur as a result of intervening word-association experiences" (Haber & Erdelyi, 1967, p. 627).

Throughout the late 1960s and 1970s, and beyond, Matthew Erdelyi continued this work, which became known as the "hypermnesia" paradigm. If amnesia represents the forgetting of information, then hypermnesia can be defined as the sudden re-membering of previously forgotten or repressed information. In fact, Erdelyi conducted an extensive series of studies, mostly at Brooklyn College of the City University of New York (e.g. Erdelyi, 1970, 1990; Erdelyi & Goldberg, 1979; Erdelyi & Kleinbard, 1978). The subsequent research used infinitely more complex methodologies which not only investigated recall memory in the laboratory situation, but also examined the growth of recall over longer periods of time in more naturalistic settings. Together, these papers represent a huge body of empirical research, which has continued to support the existence of the hypermnesia paradigm.

David S. Holmes (1990) of the University of Kansas has questioned the validity of Erdelyi's work and of much of the other experimental data on the existence of repression, in part because of the laboratory nature of the work. One could, of course, argue that a university student free-associating to a Southern scene does not necessarily reflect the situation of a putatively abused patient suddenly remembering details of a traumatic rape after free-associating on the analytic couch. Nevertheless, Erdelyi's work does most certainly substantiate Freud's claim that repressed material can return to consciousness as a result of talking. Fortunately, since Erdelyi's work, an even stronger piece of data has appeared in the literature which Holmes and others might regard as more valid and more naturalistic.

Linda Meyer Williams (1994a) of the Family Research Laboratory at the University of New Hampshire in the United States undertook research of a different nature to examine whether traumatic events can be forgotten, and whether such forgetting can actually be documented. Williams obtained medical records of 206 girls aged from 10 months to 12 years, who attended the emergency-room of a certain hospital in the United States between 1 April 1973 and 30 June 1975, as diagnosed victims of child sexual abuse. Many of these girls had, in fact, suffered from actual vaginal penetration. In 1990 and 1991, Williams managed to contact 153 of the original 206 girls, now full-grown women. She told her sample that she wanted them to participate in an interview study about "the lives and health of women who during childhood received medical care at the city hospital" (Williams, 1994a, p. 1169). The investigator did not mention child sexual abuse, or the fact that these women had been victims of child sexual abuse between 1973 and 1975. Eventually, 129 members of the sample agreed to be interviewed by Williams. The women ranged from 18 years to 31 years of age, and most of them belonged to the African American population.

Astonishingly, 38% of the sample of 129 women did not report the abuse that Williams and colleagues knew had been documented in the hospital records. Williams of course considered the possibility that these women simply did not wish to talk about such experiences to the interviewer, but she regards this as unlikely in view of the fact that these particular women revealed large amounts of extremely intimate information to the two interviewers, both of whom had received special training in speaking sensitively to survivors of childhood sexual abuse. Thus, although

Linda Williams had strong documentary evidence in her possession to prove that these women had undergone abuse as children,
a large proportion had no conscious memory of the events at all,
thus suggesting that they had repressed the memory of painful
abuse from conscious awareness, in much the same way that Little
Hans had forgotten all about his visits to Sigmund Freud. Williams
(1994a) has concluded that "These findings suggest that having no
memory of child sexual abuse is a common occurrence" (p. 1173).
At least two rebuttals of Williams's work have appeared in the
professional literature (Loftus, Garry, & Feldman, 1994; Pope &
Hudson, 1995), but Williams (1994b) has herself replied to most of
the concerns raised by her critics.

Concluding remarks

Sigmund Freud suggested that we forget material from our own
biographies in the face of overwhelming psychic calamity. We repress information to protect ourselves from remembering its awful
impact. And yet this information can return to us when we start to
talk about our experiences. All of the subjects in Matthew Erdelyi's
research improved their memories for various stimuli when they
began to free-associate; so, why should a patient in treatment not
also "suddenly" remember material during the course of a psychotherapy session? Linda Williams's study has demonstrated that
whereas some women will remember abuse after talking about
it, others will not, even though we know that abuse has really
occurred, thus complicating the picture quite considerably. The
study of human memory function remains an ongoing concern,
but at the present time it seems quite reasonable for clinicians to
conclude that it can be possible for repressed events to return to
consciousness after long periods of time, and that if our patients
begin to harbour doubts about their parents, then we ought to
listen cautiously—but listen seriously as well.

CHAPTER FIVE

False memory syndrome

Susie Orbach

*In this chapter, Susie Orbach shows the part that feminism
played in the understanding of the extent of abuse against
women and children. She examines the processes of personal
denial in the consulting-room, as well as societal denial and the
role of the media.*

In the spring of 1993, I wrote a piece in my *Guardian* column
raising concerns about the take-up in the media of the so-called
false memory syndrome. I expressed my surprise and concern
that so many column inches were being devoted to a discussion of
parents claiming to be unjustly accused by their children rather
than to what I considered the more serious problem of the sexual
violation of children.

I argued that—as Jeffrey Masson (1984), Judith Herman Lewis
(Herman, 1981, 1992), and others have argued—psychoanalysis
has a complex and reasonably dishonourable history in relation to
the acceptance of the veracity of reports of childhood sexual abuse.
Since Freud abandoned the seduction theory in the late 1890s and
transferred his understanding of the accounts of his patients' childhood memories of sexual encounters with parents to the realm of

internal phantasy, psychotherapy and its allied fields have tended to overlook both the existence and the real trauma of sexual abuse.

When women began to claim for themselves the right to speak of their own experience, they could articulate what life was like from their vantage point. They described how work, mothering, relationships, the health system, the education system looked to them, how the interface between the public world and the private world of the family operated, how their intimate relationships functioned or didn't function, how there were pressures on them to be the emotional support system and emotional sewage-treatment plant for everyone. Once these perceptions were given space so that women's subjective experience could be described and validated, it was possible to create the kind of climate in the general population that meant that women could reveal secrets they had kept about some of the emotional and sexual violence that they had sustained in their childhood.

As women came forward to testify to the brutality that they lived with, it became obvious that childhood sexual abuse was far more widespread than common sense had allowed one to think. Women's recognition of their own history and the valuing of women's lives, which had begun to be on the agenda over the last twenty years, led in turn to a recognition that children's experiences needed to be valued and recognized too, and there was a shift in how we perceived children. Children were no longer simply the possessions of their parents but citizens with rights, including the right to be heard and a right to a childhood free of abuse.

This shift in the way in which children were regarded led to people listening more to children, just as we began to listen more to women. Out of the mouths of young children—both girls and boys—came horrific reports of deeply inappropriate sexual, violent, and sadistic relationships foisted on them, and as a society we were required to think about what on earth was going on. It became obvious that many children were surviving in perilous situations and that they were embedded in dangerous and hurtful relationships. Child protection workers and doctors moved in in various ways to safeguard the children, and a public conversation about the level of sexual abuse ensued.

This public conversation is marked by a great deal of passion and hysteria. There are many parties to the conversation, although they are not often all heard, and the debate is often characterized by a kind of political fundamentalism—"All men are potential abusers" or "The children just make up what they want the adults to hear". But in truth there are other voices straining to be heard and straining to understand and position themselves vis-à-vis these polarities. For many, the idea of sexual abuse is so repellent and so unfathomable that its wide-scale existence is incomprehensible: to accept that so many have been violated forces a deep reconsideration of human behaviour. It challenges their sense of what it means to be human. For others, a certain kind of abuse can be accepted where another kind is negated. Colleagues of mine, for example, will say, "Yes, I accept sexual abuse . . . but ritual abuse— now, that is just not on. Are you sure you aren't being bamboozled here or getting over-involved?" For others, confusion, fear, and conflicting feelings overwhelm them, and the public discussion with its fundamentalist demands makes it hard for them to talk.

In my *Guardian* column, I wrote that an interesting phenomenon from my perspective as a clinician—as a general psychotherapist rather than someone who works in the area of sexual abuse—is the discomfort and resistance that I observe when my clients or patients encounter in themselves evidence of sexual abuse in their childhood. They tell of it, but then withdraw from the knowledge of what they have said. Unlike children who are in the midst of an abusive situation, adults who appeared to have been abused in childhood, far from rushing off to accuse their parents, were extremely hesitant to acknowledge what might be staring us both in the face. They would do anything to conceal this knowledge from themselves. They would rather not know, not confront their history, not believe.

I speculated that, if the survivors were amnesic, then it was possible that the perpetrators—many of whom had been consistently abused themselves when children—were similarly amnesic or dissociated when they were committing acts of sexual abuse. I did not say this to let them off the hook, but to extend insights from clinical practice with survivors. I return to this issue of secrecy and resistance to the acknowledgement of abuse shortly in more detail. For the moment, I want to take you through my experience and thinking following the publication of my *Guardian* piece.

The piece came out, and I was besieged by correspondence from parents who alleged that they had been accused, falsely, by their children of sexual abuse. My first response was to think that I had seriously underestimated the phenomenon. To be sure, I had acknowledged in the article that it was possible that parents were being falsely accused, but I set this within the context that the main issue was the abuse of children and I questioned whether the focus on false memory was not some kind of backlash both against feminism and a response to our inability as a culture to deal with the horror of child molestation. I also wondered why adult children would be accusing their parents falsely. Like the therapist I am, my thought was that if sexual abuse had not occurred, then something had gone dreadfully wrong for the children to have turned in this manner against their parents. We know that there can be deep conflict between parents and children, but for a child to express that conflict through a false allegation of sexual abuse struck me as indicative of something quite serious.

So the letters arrived, and my assistant Petra Fried and I read them. Some of these letters were extremely moving. All were deeply upsetting because they detailed fractured relationships in which the parents were inexplicably bereft of a relationship with their children. The letters fell into two camps: those that struck one as the absolutely genuine outpourings of broken-hearted parents, and those that disquieted me in a different way. The latter read as wooden—one might almost say they were formulaically composed. Although we did not decipher this in all of the letters in this category, there were certainly some containing slips ("I did abuse my daughter" when the writer intended "I didn't abuse my daughter"), which was extremely interesting, and all included a curious reference to the fact that the writers were not anti-feminist.

I determined to keep an open mind and to accept that I had seriously underestimated the number of parents falsely accused. I felt that there was incontrovertible evidence that some people trained in hypnotherapy were using suggestion to induce an explanation of sexual abuse for the distress that their patients came to them with. I was prepared to consider that people were more suggestible than perhaps I had realized and that false memory was something to be grappled with.

This was one strain of my thinking, and during the rest of the year I encountered many people who would want to reinforce that line of argument. At the same time, I was concerned to discover how many people in my professional and wider personal world dismissed the relevance of sexual abuse and called those who worried about it zealots or perverts themselves.

But a meeting with Roger Scotford on television has continued to worry me about the British False Memory Society and its influence in generating articles like the Simon Hoggart piece in *The Observer* of 23 March 1994 which argued that rational argument is impossible. Hoggart has likened the pressure on parents falsely accused to the "Red Scare" that swept North America in the 1950s. Such articles promote the idea that the sexual abuse of children is secondary to the major problem of false memory.

I left the BBC studio feeling very uneasy about some of the membership of his organization, and I was alarmed to see academics and psychoanalysts joining his advisory board. It did not seem parallel to parents and academics who join organizations such as SANE or MENCAP.

Since then, Valerie Sinason's brave and deeply disturbing collection *Treating Survivors of Satanist Abuse* (1994) has been published, and we have seen a new round of denial and dismissal that such things can happen. BBC2's Newsnight, in trying to deal with the question of child abuse, promised those they wished to interview—the agencies and individuals involved with the aftercare of survivors—a non-biased programme. The result was far from that—it was as partisan as one could possibly go in the direction of proclaiming false memory to be the fundamental problem, not sexual abuse.

Those who work in child protection and with those who have been abused must suffer appalling feelings of outrage and helplessness as they see mendaciously mischaracterized as fantasy what we know to be happening. It is as though what had to be kept secret, what had to be denied, what could not be spoken of by the children was now being done on a public level. The truth of sexual abuse had pierced the façade of civility, and that was so threatening to everyone that it had to be denied once again.

Five years on from that initial piece in which my thinking was challenged at every point, I have come back to—or forward to—thinking what I wrote then. That is to say, we cannot bear to take on the reality of childhood sexual abuse because it is so awful, so undermining, so emblematic of the deep cultural crisis that we are in. We prefer not to think of it, not to believe it, not to envision that such practices are part of our cultural life. If we accept that they are, then we have to re-draw the way in which we understand human relationships. We have to extend our analysis to account for the frequency rather than the deviance of these practices.

* * *

Let us look for a moment at the impact of secrecy in both the public and the private domain and how in the individual situation this has a bearing on the psychic structure of a woman who had been abused as a child.

Part of why so much of this only reluctantly comes out in the clinical situation is that it keeps the secret of the original abusing relationship, in which the perpetrator made it clear to the victim that the activities that he (or she) engaged in were never to be revealed. The need to keep a secret, the very fact that the abuse could not be disclosed, has meant that the abused person has had to find a way to cope with this traumatic experience in an abnormal way. Usually, if we are traumatized by a death or an accident or a mugging, we try to work through that experience both cognitively and affectively. That is to say, we try talking about it, we endeavour to understand it, and we go through a process in which mourning, rage, grief, horror, terror, and so on are experienced in a reasonably supported context. Not so with sexual abuse. The very fact that the person was sworn to secrecy or knew by the emotional ambience of the surrounds of the abuse that secrecy was an important element of it, and the fact that there was indeed no one to turn to who would listen to an account of the abuse and stop it, means that, for many survivors, by the time they get to adulthood they have had to banish it from their conscious or aware self or they will be driven mad by the pain and knowledge of what they have lived through. Their psyche needs to accommodate two concurrent phenomena. First, it needs to find a way to deal with deeply destructive experience. Second, it needs to find a way to conceal the knowledge of these experiences from others.

What becomes obvious in working with survivors is that much of their life has to be lived in their head because the outside world is a very dangerous place. It is as though they have had to withdraw energy from the real people and relationships in their lives and try to construct scenarios that make plausible, make comprehensible, the fact of the abuse that they have experienced. When the psyche cannot deal with excruciating pain directly, when it cannot speak of it, it has to find ways to account for what has happened that leave the person functioning. One of the ways it does this is that it creates an inner world in which things work out rather differently. There are several processes at work which I will mention because they impact upon the kinds of problems that can occur in the therapeutic relationship.

The first of these processes usually involves the person who has been abused rewriting the events in such a way as to place himself or herself as the central actor in the abuse, that is to say, renders himself or herself as culpable, as though he or she were somehow at fault for what has happened or is happening. Now this may seem bizarre—that the victim turns herself or himself into an instigator—but if we think of the feelings of powerless and helplessness that we all find incredibly difficult and we multiply them several-fold, and we imagine ourselves to be living in a situation that is already too dangerous to disclose and so we are insecure to begin with and have the experience of being disregarded, we can see that a psychically lethal combination of low self-esteem and the psyche's inability to contain feelings of defencelessness creates a push to escape in fantasy from the situation by creating a scenario that has a get-out clause—in other words, by making oneself somehow at fault. If one is at fault, then one could somehow find a way to stop. One is potentially power*ful* rather than power*less*. This reversal of what is, momentarily soothes the pain of powerlessness and creates a sense in the person that he or she is not without resources or possibilities for escape.

Now the difficulty with this scenario—apart from, of course, its inaccuracy and the harm that it does the person—is that in a therapy relationship this survival mechanism, this taking on of the fault, is very hard to dislodge. The reason is that in order to dislodge it one is asking the client to give up the defence that she has constructed, one is suggesting that she can manage the despair, helplessness, rage, and so on that has been repressed, and she, of course, does not feel that she can. In the therapy, in wishing to respect the client one can also feel as though one is tempted to engage in a tug-of-war, with the client inviting one in, as she discloses a little, and then her shutting the therapist and herself out as she reconstructs the scenario in which she is an instigator. This is a frustrating process because good therapeutic practice demands that she be able to feel, to take on board her experience of the abuse, at a pace that is manageable.

As a therapist one may wish to be more powerful in return, so that when we say "Look, this happened to you and you were vulnerable, and you couldn't do anything about it, and that is what we have to face together, the fact of what happened, the pain of what happened and so on", we want to be doing magic. We want our words to clear away the psychic distortions that she has created, but they can't, and so we too feel deeply impotent.

Allied to the taking on of culpability is the identification that many survivors unconsciously make with their abusers. In its most extreme form, it is as though there are sub-personalities to the survivor which she may or may not know about. They may emerge during the course of therapy, so that at one moment or in part of a session one will be dealing with an aspect of self who is a compliant or sweet little girl, at another with a dissociated part who is an angry, wilful, destructive little witch, or else a hateful, abusive, and manipulative part. None of these part selves or separate personalities are necessarily truer than others. There may be a central self that complies with social norms, keeps down a job, looks after the kids, and so on, but there may be subsidiary selves, known or unknown to the central self, that undermine and ridicule whatever she is able to achieve (Davies & Frawley, 1994; Herman, 1992).

Now the difficulty for the therapist is that firstly he or she may not know about these separate selves for a long time, and when they do come out they may break all conventional boundaries in ways that the therapist feels unprepared for. They will press demands on the therapist for extra kinds of caretaking, which invite a breaking of therapeutic boundaries. I am thinking here of the pressure on the therapist to see the person several extra times a week, take telephone calls at ungodly hours, let the person move into the therapist's own home, give her money, and so on. These kinds of pressures are not uncommon for therapists working with survivors of sexual abuse. If there is a place to discuss the pressure that the therapist feels under, then he or she will be more able to provide a creative answer; often, however, the therapist gets drawn into a feeling that the urgency of the client's situation is misunderstood and that colleagues are being too rigid, and so the therapist withdraws from talking about the pressure, accedes to breaking boundaries in an unhelpful manner, and then becomes drawn into the client's drama in such a way that he or she is forced eventually to disappoint her, prove untrustworthy, and reiterate at a psychological level the experience of being let down that the client needs to work through rather than re-enact.

The pressure to re-enact at an emotional level is, of course, part of what occurs in any therapy, and that pressure and the ability to understand it and work through it with the client is central to the process of therapy. With survivors, where the pressure is so forcefully turned up, it is crucial that there are supervisory sessions where this pressure can be discussed rather than the therapy becoming a secret re-enactment or acting out.

I was saying that one of the psychic consequences of the splitting-off of indigestible experience is the identification that the client may unconsciously make with her perpetrator. This identification can have many forms, but the particularly troublesome ones occur when the therapist feels as though she or he is being abused in the therapy relationship. This is a difficult thing to talk about, but it does seem to be a reasonably common occurrence in therapy, and many therapists and workers, if given have a chance, talk about feeling guilty and confused about their experience of feeling abused and used by the clients. It is not in the actual things that are said but in a kind of emotional ambience that they feel is created in which the therapist comes to feel through the process of projective identification a version of what the client felt. The client finds an emotional way to communicate what she felt and feels at a non-verbal level about being abused. Along with the capacity to arouse these feelings in the therapist, there is also a counterpart in that the therapist can feel sadistic in return and can identify with the sadism and cruelty of the perpetrator. We are now learning that such feelings and responses are perfectly expectable in therapy with people who have survived what seems like the unsurvivable.

In our work with survivors, we face many problems. A consequence of the abuse is that the person we are working with may never have experienced relationships that are not marked by abuse; alternative relationships, relationships that are not characterized by abuse, have very few psychological channels to go down. In other words, if the relationships on which a person is meant to rely have forsaken her in treacherous ways, then she learns that relationships are perilous. So if mother has betrayed us by allowing our father, brother, step-father, uncle, grandpa, neighbour to abuse us consistently, or if mother herself has been a perpetrator of abuse, then we understand that relationship means abuse. We do not have an emotional alternative framework. We may read about hearts and flowers relationships, see them on television, but our own imprinted experience is of betrayal. But this betrayal, with the meagre relationship it offered, may have been the only relationship that was given to us, so to desert it, to abandon the structure of this kind of relationship, to disavow this form of relating, is almost impossible because as *the* model for relationship and the central relationship it is still desperately needed.

This need and this pattern then shapes other relationships, so that when a relationship that is not abusive is offered—such as a therapy relationship—it may appear to the person as abusive; and if it does not turn out to be abusive, the person may find herself so confused that she tries to shape this relationship in line with relationships that she has known. The struggle to reshape what relationship can mean, the need to bear witness to profound horror, the attempt to help the survivor put the culpability where it really belongs, the need to resist the narcissistic pull to be the one person who can save this person's life all make working with survivors both very difficult, very moving, and profoundly rewarding. But to do it we need to be listened to as well. We need mini-versions of the space that we give our clients, so that we can process together the horror that we have learnt about without repressing it in turn.

* * *

Sexual abuse is a horrifying aspect of daily life for many people. It constitutes a war on our children, it pollutes their lives, and it exercises a chilling effect on the rest of us. I, for one, would rather not believe it. I want to deny its prevalence and reserve its particular horror as the misfortune of the few. I want to applaud and valourize those who survive. Like anyone else, I want the stories to be inaccurate; emotionally, I wish that false memory were a phenomenon that I could believe in. It would relieve me of the burden of accepting the wide-scale nature of child abuse. But I can't. Yes, false memory can occur; yes, there are rotten therapists and so-called healers out there. But to focus on that is to discharge us of the responsibility of understanding the conditions that create sexual abuse and absolve us of the need to work to change the structure of relationships that produces them.

I am at a loss to understand how sexual abuse can occur on such a wide scale, but I do accept that it does. I cannot theorize the whys. I can only comment on the practice and the reactions that I observe in those who have been abused—as well as the reactions of us who haven't—to the fact of abuse. In my incomprehension, I struggle to understand the clinical implications and consequences of abuse. I know that others, some of whom are workers in the field of sexual abuse, are better able to theorize the whys. But just because we find it hard to accept and hard to comprehend, it does not mean that we should take the easy way out and focus our attention on something that we can get a hold of—false memory. That is a problem, to be sure. But we need to devote our efforts to confronting why we, as a culture, can tolerate the sexual abuse and torture of children.

CHAPTER SIX

"What if I should die?"

Jennifer Johns

In this chapter, Jennifer Johns describes the terrible physical countertransference impact on an analyst listening to a patient talk of systemic savage abuse in childhood. This raises the complex issue of truth in the consulting-room.

A psychoanalyst, not young or inexperienced and to the best of her knowledge in perfect health, was sitting very still and listening to an extremely distressed patient speaking with great difficulty, of memories implying savage, perverse, and systematic many-layered cruelty in childhood.

During the story, the analyst suddenly developed pain in her own chest. The pain was central, and gradually became severe enough to make her seriously anxious about herself and to prevent her ordinary concentration on what was happening in the session. She began to try to recollect old fragments of her training in medicine as the pain spread upwards into her jaw, and she became more and more frightened that she was having a heart attack. She tried to reassure herself that the pain, though acute, was not typically cardiac, and intellectually she tried to make sense of it in the naive hope that, once made sense of, it would go away. Unable to listen to or concentrate on her patient, she told herself that it was probably indigestion, or not in fact real, and chided herself for failing her patient at such a vital moment. She told herself that she must pull herself together and return to her concentration on the patient and the session, and that until the pain went down her left arm she would not interrupt the session. However, she was very frightened.

On another level, the analyst's mental conflict was acute too, since even in the midst of the fear and pain she recognized that what she had been hearing, and had stopped being able to hear, was a story carrying the implication of the most barbaric human behaviour—the most horrifying that she had heard in twenty years of analytic practice—and she found herself beginning to doubt her own ego-strength when discovering the inability to listen to it and to realize that it was possible that, in putting her through this physical ordeal, her body was refusing to allow her to submit herself to the psychological one of taking in what her patient was saying. It was not the first time that the story had been told, but on each occasion further details of dehumanizing and debasing perversity emerged, and the patient had needed time and space to be able to reach the thoughts about them.

There are, of course, occasions when listening to a patient that an analyst (and the analyst was, of course, myself) may quite consciously feel a wish not to hear, a wish to keep some memory, thought, or fantasy out of the mind, and afterwards a knowledge that what one has just heard about is something that, given the choice, one would rather not have known, thoughts that cannot be unthought, memories that cannot be unremembered, words that must always leave a trace, ineradicable evidence of the most deliberately cruel and perverse elements of human life. An analyst, however, in offering a mind to others, to receive their thoughts and memories and fantasies, must therefore have some optimism about his or her own mental strength and capacity to survive such onslaughts, especially when trying to help those who have not psychologically survived. In my turmoil, I accused myself of arrogance, of having held a naive presumption that in my professional life I could take anything, manage any material that my patient might give me. I felt that I was facing, as well as the reality of failing my patient so badly, the humiliation of failing my own ego-ideal, and, as well as the shocks associated with what I had heard and was being asked to believe, I was shocked at how badly my own body was letting me down.

All psychoanalysts are used to the everyday analytic task of the examination of their own inner world alongside that of their patients, the examination of their own thoughts and feelings, and the everlasting and recurrent psychoanalytic question as to the relationship between their own inner world and that of their patients, the conscious and unconscious influences of each upon the other. By the term countertransference is understood something rather different and complementary—the influence, frequently unconsciously experienced, of the patient's transference to the analyst upon the analyst. The analyst knows to watch for countertransferences, in so far as that is possible during analytic sessions, countertransference being so largely unconscious, sometimes so unconscious that its existence may be manifested by bodily sensations, and analysts are also used to the phenomenon of recognizing with hindsight how their own countertransferences can affect a session—there are times when patients point that out directly and clearly, and times when it is possible to puzzle it out for oneself. There are also times when it is appropriate to share particularly obscure problems with a colleague; on this particular occasion, there were reasons why this had not, in fact, been possible. These situations were familiar, but what had happened on this day was a new phenomenon. I had never, so far as I could remember, experienced such an overwhelmingly painful and frightening bodily response to a patient, or felt so terrifyingly helpless and in real and imminent danger of death. A certain common sense told me that it is not impossible to become ill in terms of physical reality, and that illness can strike at any time without necessarily being related to the patient, and warned me against a kind of magical thinking involving a denial of my own mortality, but I did not find this

WHAT IF I SHOULD DIE?"

convincing—the immediacy of the physical response was too closely related to the patient's material to be, I felt, accidental.

In calmer moments, it is possible to recall that by means of what is called projective identification an analyst's internal state can reflect either the affects of the patient as the subject in the situation being remembered or dealt with, or the affects of the patient's object in that situation—and work with traumatized patients leads one to know that not only is terrible pain, fear, and suffering traumatic, but so too is the utter helplessness of being a victim, and, moreover, that the further helplessness of being either unable to help another victim or of believing oneself in some way responsible for the other's suffering is cumulatively traumatic. These pieces of everyday professional knowledge were, however, unavailable in the acute moment. When I recovered, much later, it was possible to think out the occurrence more calmly and to realize that the helplessness, pain, and fear felt might indeed have been related to the overwhelming experience that the patient had been describing, which had contained elements of all these. Surprised most of all by the bodily phenomenon, I later wondered whether the pain was due to my own oesophagus having gone into spasm as a physical attempt to defend myself against swallowing the patient's material. Swallowing would mean acceptance of it, and I recognized the very strong wish not to accept such evidence of human perverse cruelty. It may be important to state that although with this person there had been times earlier in the treatment when I had found myself questioning what I heard, I had in fact reached a stage when that intellectual barrier was past. My mind could picture all too well—but it made me feel very ill, and very frightened.

It is the job of a psychoanalyst to help the sufferer make sense of a frightening and confusing inner world, and, in order to do that, the analyst must be able to understand something of the fears and confusions of that inner world. Those fears and confusions are frequently, though not always, related to perceptions of the outer world, and those perceptions are, of course, received by a perceptual apparatus with a developmental history of its own. The perceptual apparatus itself may have been damaged and distorted during that development, even to the extent of being unable to perceive an event, or the memory of an event, in the same way that another, less distorted person might. When an analyst listens to a patient speaking about unbearable pain or communicating it by non-verbal or even unconscious communication, as in projective identification, the analyst must hope that the experience will be bearable by himself or herself. That will mean containing the experience, processing it, and eventually being able, with the patient, to put it into words in such a way that the patient can accept it.

What happens when the flood of feeling from the patient makes the analyst unable to think or contain the experience? This may be sharing the patient's historical state of having been overwhelmed, but it is of no use at all in making sense of it. It would be easy to say, and perhaps true, that I, the analyst in question, was myself inadequately analysed, that had I known myself better I might have been more able to contain the situation of horror presented to me. However, the catalogue of human cruelty is very long, and, while one may be prepared for many of its entries, particularly those based on intimate two-body relationships or even the kind of institutionalized torture of a concentration camp, each of which can have its own bizarre rationality, the organized distortion of reason that is entered under the label "evil" is different. Systematic perversion of all values, which overturns all expectation of predictable response in favour of the savage joy of perversity—by which I mean annihilation of all that is good, for the sake of that destruction only—is painful and difficult to hear. Those who habitually work with such material agree on the need for colleague support and limitation of exposure to it, to protect themselves. It is also important that any colleagues consulted to help deal with and accept these things have experience of having tried themselves to help similar distress, so that the initial barrier of acceptance of the horror of the extremes of human cruelty is passed.

It seems that very young infants already need to make sense of the happenings in themselves and their environment by means of creating a narrative for themselves, as a way of making some sort of order or sense of the phenomena observed and experienced, and this would seem to be related to the beginning of the epistemophilic drive to understand, to find out, to master confusion by knowing. Perhaps those who find the world most confusing develop into the most insistently curious, if they are not too daunted by their confusion or inhibited by the environment's response to it. The question of when, and to what degree, curiosity and the need to establish mental order and a narrative (or, when older, a search for an actual explanation of confusing data) may be defensive against too-frightening confusion is an interesting one. The need to know, the need to establish so-called historical truth, may be a defence against overwhelming affect. Amongst our other defences when we feel utterly helpless, we may take refuge in an attempt at mental mastery, so that even in suffering pain or defeat we are comforted in that we can at least understand the mind of the person who caused it. This creates the kind of situation in which an about-to-be executed victim forgives his torturers in another version of "Father, forgive them . . ."

Among the attempts at self-preservation there is a wish in human beings—and this includes those who become analysts—to establish, or be able to establish, the veridicality of new information. In an analyst, this may be defensive, for a search for "facts" can allow distance from the reality of the psychic pain of the sufferer. It may feel much safer to escape into the outside world where "facts" are felt to be verifiable, solid matters. However, such an escape is a betrayal of the analytic task, which is to understand the inner world of the patient, especially *in extremis*. For those in contact with the world that requires facts, the legal or protective world, this can be a nightmare—one aspect of their professional world needs something called proof, another needs understanding of inner pain, and the two may be antithetical.

For myself, there is no way that the experience of having suffered the fear for my very life that occurred with my patient could in any way be called to account as legal proof of anything. I am safe from that requirement. I am left with an enormous question— to what extent was my own terrifying experience in any way validating of my patient's inner world? My answer to that question is that it is. It was important that my understanding of the inner position should happen. It seemed to me that my very body answered my patient. I did not want to know the extent of the experience—and the patient had been very sparing of detail, very careful to dose my exposure to it—and I believe that in the end my body tried to refuse it.

What happened next? My patient, in fact, noticed my distress and ended the session early, also distressed at the effect on me. For many later sessions, the effect was discussed and the fear of causing my death became paramount. The quality of work altered, and the elaboration of the story was delayed. The patient retreated into a different way of working, and the issue, for the moment, changed. I regretted my failure, though I could not have avoided it, and the question of the repetition of past failures came into prominence.

Though this very frightening experience has never, I am glad to say, been repeated, I do class it as a manifestation of bodily countertransference, as a communication from my patient of the extreme overwhelming by fear of death, guilt, and horror.

The question of veridicality, of the search for so-called historical truth, is a matter for lawyers and the police. Analysts must know that when a patient brings material of great anguish, the analyst is hearing a true story of anguish.

CHAPTER SEVEN

False memory syndrome movements: the origins and the promoters

Marjorie Orr

In this chapter, Marjorie Orr focuses on a few of the complex facts in the lives of some of the key figures in the international false memory societies. This throws light on the origins of the movement and explains some of the ethical difficulties involved.

To begin at the beginning. The man credited with having coined the term "false memory syndrome" is an American, Dr Ralph Underwager, who was one of the co-founders of the False Memory Syndrome Foundation (FMSF), along with his wife, Hollida Wakefield, and Pamela and Peter Freyd, in March 1992 in Philadelphia. In 1993, Underwager gave an interview, with his wife, to a Dutch paedophile magazine, *Paedika* (Geraci, 1993). In the article, *Paedika* reported him as saying that paedophilia could be seen as a responsible choice and that having sex with children could be seen as "part of God's will". He has said that he was not misquoted by the magazine, which is a self-styled journal of paedophilia and prints articles such as "Man–Boy Sexual Relationships in Cross-Cultural Perspective", "A Crush on My Girl

Scout Leader", " The World Is Bursting with Adults so I Am Always Pleased to See a Little Girl", and "The Hysteria over Child Pornography and Paedophilia". However, he does say that when the quotes are used that they are out of context and that he is against child abuse.

Underwager's interview also argued that paedophiles trying to decriminalize child sex could be compared to Christ struggling up to Calvary, and that feminists were jealous of men's ability to bond with boys. It has recently been reprinted in full in a new book, *Dares to Speak: Historical and Contemporary Perspective on Boy-Love*, edited by Joseph Geraci (1997), editor of *Paidika*, the Dutch paedophile magazine in which the interview first appeared.

Underwager has for years been an "expert witness" for the defence of accused molesters in cases in the United States and in the United Kingdom. He gave evidence to the Cleveland Inquiry in 1987. In April 1994, U.S. Appeal Court judges threw out at a preliminary stage a defamation suit that he had raised against Anna Salter, a child psychologist, who had written a highly critical exposé of his scholarship and methods (Salter, 1991). The judges paraphrased the views in Underwager and Wakefield's two books, *The Real World of Child Interrogations* (1990) and *Accusations of Child Sexual Abuse* (Wakefield & Underwager, 1988), as indicating that most accusations of child sexual abuse stem from memories implanted by faulty clinical techniques rather than from sexual contact between children and adults.[1] The judges commented: "The books have not been well received in the medical and scientific press." Later: "Underwager's approach has failed to carry the medical profession, but it has endeared him to defense lawyers."

The three judges said that Anna Salter was not malicious in concluding that Underwager was "a hired gun who makes a living by deceiving judges about the state of medical knowledge and thus assisting child molesters to evade punishment". They were clear that the law would not challenge her in continuing to say so. In 1993, a Canadian Court similarly found Underwager's testimony "replete with misinterpretation, misquoting and reliance upon information that is not empirical data". They rejected his expert witness testimony as biased, found his manner and demeanour "argumentative and at times condescending and insulting", and also took exception to his assertion that he had not

been disqualified before: "Dr. Underwager's continuation in saying that he was not so disqualified can only be interpreted as a
deliberate attempt to mislead the Court."

After the appearance of the *Paedika* interview, Dr. Underwager
resigned from the FMSF board. His wife, Hollida Wakefield, co-
author of his books, who said in the *Paedika* interview that she
thought it would be "nice" to do a long-term research study with
"100 twelve year old boys in relationships with loving paedophiles", remains on the FMSF board.

The other co-founders of the FMSF, Pamela and Peter Freyd,
are middle-class parents who describe themselves as innocents,
much maligned—the father, a mathematician, having been accused privately by one of his two adult daughters of abusing her in
childhood.

The American media gave them almost unquestioning support
until their daughter, Professor Jennifer Freyd, a cognitive psychology expert in her 30s, reluctantly and painfully felt obliged to
speak up publicly to stop the damage that she felt that her parents
and their organization were doing to abuse victims (Freyd, 1993).

She spoke not of the core "recovered memories" themselves,
which she rightly felt to be private, but of the parts of childhood
that she clearly remembered in which she had felt that sexual
boundaries were constantly crossed and in which she felt invaded,
controlled, intimidated, and manipulated.

In this her one public lecture, she told a family story in which
her parents grew up—effectively—as step brother and sister from
a young age. Their own parents had had an affair that culminated
after eleven years in marriage, at which time Pamela and Peter
Freyd also married aged 18 and 20. Professor Freyd recollected her
father speaking openly of his own childhood homosexual liaison
as an 11-year-old with a paedophile artist. She remembered being
made to dance nude in front of him aged 9 with a friend, and of
being taught to kiss on the mouth "like an adult" for a school play,
at the age of 11, in front of the cast. She made particular mention of
a mould of his penis and testicles, which she saw on one occasion
on the mantelpiece in the sitting-room. She says he continually
made sexual comments, which were regarded as normal in the
family: for example, he said that the family dog could sense her
sister's sexual interest in men, and he explained in front of his 2-

year-old grandson that turkey basters were used by lesbians to inseminate themselves. He drank heavily through her childhood and was hospitalized for alcoholism.

None of this is proof of actual sexual abuse but it certainly raises serious questions about what did go on in a seemingly disturbed family. Jennifer Freyd herself, though highly motivated as a student, did suffer from promiscuity, anorexia, drug abuse, and feelings of guilt, shame, and terror. Both Pamela and Peter Freyd now deny that the family was dysfunctional. The other sister and Peter Freyd's brother (his only sibling) both support Jennifer Freyd. None of them is in direct contact with the parents.

Peter Freyd's brother, William, recently wrote an open letter to a TV station after a slanted documentary on recovered memories. He said:

> There is no doubt in my mind that there was severe abuse in the home of Peter and Pam, while they were raising their daughters. . . . The False Memory Syndrome Foundation is a fraud designed to deny a reality that Peter and Pam have spent most of their lives trying to escape. . . . That the False Memory Syndrome Foundation has been able to excite so much media attention has been a great surprise to those of us who would like to admire and respect the objectivity of people in the media. Neither Peter's mother (who was also mine), nor his daughters, nor me have wanted anything to do with Peter and Pam for periods of time ranging up to more than two decades. We do not understand why you would "buy" such a flawed story.[2]

Jennifer Freyd also emphasized in her lecture (Freyd, 1993) that she did not recover her memories under hypnosis. She went to a mainstream clinical psychologist in a medical practice, and the memories started to emerge after the second session. Yet she said: "Apparently my mother has suggested to many people that my memories were the result of therapeutic intervention, even hypnosis. This makes me wonder about the claims of other parents associated with FMSF. . . . It is as if the weight of a whole Foundation (False Memory Syndrome) stands behind my mother's frenzied denial of my reality."

Fourteen months after the original private accusation of abuse, Pamela Freyd incorporated the False Memory Syndrome Foundation. It has been said that this organization grew out of one family's feud that has overgrown its boundaries and come into the popular culture.

Indeed, Jennifer Freyd's father wrote to her (Freyd, 1993): "I still insist on thinking of our Newsletter, indeed the whole project, as being primarily a way of communicating with our daughters." Quite bizarrely, it had not occurred to him that she would resent "the extent to which we have gone public". He was surprised that she turned down the chance to become an advisor to the Foundation.

At the time, Pamela Freyd, the present FMSF chairperson, said of Underwager and Wakefield that "there are not enough words to thank (them) . . . for the loving professional support that they have given to the FMS Foundation to help us become an independent organization. We would not exist without them" (FMS Foundation Newsletter, 29 February 1992).

Professor Jennifer Freyd recently published a book called *Betrayal Trauma: The Logic of Forgetting Childhood Abuse* (1996). In it she argues that "under certain conditions, such as abuse by a close caregiver, amnesia for the abuse is an adaptive response, for amnesia may allow a dependent child to remain attached to—and thus elicit at least some degree of life-sustaining nurturing and protection from—his or her abusive caregiver" (p. 180).

The *New York Times Book Review* described the book as a "thoughtful, judicious and thorough scholarly analysis of a subject that has generated more heat than light . . . her work serves as a salutary reminder that if treated as serious science rather than media hoopla, the recovered memory debate could provide a significant window on mind–brain relationships" (Bickerton, 1997, pp. 20–21).

In the United Kingdom, the British False Memory Society (BFMS) was set up by Roger Scotford, an ex naval engineer, who has recently publicly admitted that he was accused by two of his three daughters of abusing them. In various press interviews initially under different pseudonyms—"Tony", "James", "Bill"—he says that he had a happy and involved relationship with the family throughout childhood and beyond. Only when his middle daughter went to a homeopath for an unrelated problem (thrush) did any thought of abuse arise. From this, he concluded that she was brainwashed by the therapist. He vehemently denies any abuse took place.

Talking to the two daughters involved, a different story emerges. Both insist that they were significantly unhappy throughout childhood. Recurring descriptions are of being lonely, numb, cut off, very depressed, and on occasions wanting to die. One describes herself as "the one who did not exist". Both insist it was not a family unit.

The middle daughter did go to a mainstream analyst in her late teens for about six months. On relating a sexual dream about her father, she was told that this was a perfectly normal fantasy for girls to have. When she was 27, she was invited by her father to go on a five-day holiday. Because she wanted to understand why she disliked him and to resolve their differences, she agreed. On arrival, she discovered that only one bedroom had been booked, with twin beds. She was made extremely tense by the situation. Although nothing physical happened during the holiday, she was conscious of her body beginning to react strangely.

Quite coincidentally she had in the following week booked an appointment with a homeopath for the thrush which has, along with kidney and urethral infections, been a recurring problem for most of her life. When she arrived very agitated by her holiday experience, she was greeted, she said, by the first person in her life who really wanted to listen to her. "It was completely unprompted what I came up with", she said. As with Jennifer Freyd there was no hypnotherapy. That was the start of a long, difficult process of recovering what she believed to be memories of abuse. Six years on, and out of any kind of therapy, she is standing by her story. Her younger sister is equally adamant. Neither is in contact with their father.

The Scotford story is in certain respects very like the Freyds—a family lacking good boundaries and a sense of privacy; parents "remembering" a happy time, whereas two of the three children remember the reverse; therapy being almost certainly a red herring in the argument. As with Professor Jennifer Freyd, both the Scotford girls felt (and feel) very attacked by their parent(s)'s public campaign of denial. None of them wishes to take a public platform, but they have felt pressured into making a statement.

Since Accuracy about Abuse was formed in April 1994, some adult children whose parents are members of the British False Memory Society have come forward privately to be heard. These parents' one sided stories have appeared on television and in press features. These adult children tell stories, leaving aside any abuse allegations, that indicate enmeshed families in which over-control was the norm. Their parent(s) are described as weak and pettily vindictive, possessive, and invasive. The "false memory" here again would appear to be the deluded parent's notion of an idyllically contented family life.

These adult children are for the most part fairly frightened of coming forward, and some have changed their addresses to escape their parents' clutches. None of them wishes to be involved in a public slanging match of their parent's making. Tellingly, some had never forgotten their memories and yet their parents still insist to the press that these are "false memories" implanted by a therapist. None of these adult children whom I have met recovered their memories under hypnosis. They are courageously putting together a life for themselves away from an obviously damaging childhood. They stick determinedly and sadly to their stories despite facing very distressing public attacks on themselves in television and newspaper stories and flat denial from their parent or parents. Happily, in some cases there is support from a divorced parent, and in other cases from siblings or other relatives. Several have expressed to me a feeling that the false memory syndrome movement has become for their parents just another way of attacking them or their therapists who are their support.

Membership figures for both the U.S. and the British false memory associations are regularly exaggerated in the media. Peter Freyd publicly admitted in 1995 that the paid membership for the American FMSF is around 2,500, not 16,000 as was widely thought. Similarly, Roger Scotford has said that at December 1994 the BFMS had 230 paid members, not 650 as had been quoted. The 1995 British Psychological Society report, which supported the idea that both repressed memory of sexual abuse and false memory were real occurrences, found the BFMS's membership files to be sketchy and inconsistent (Morton et al., 1995, pp. 20–21); in three-quarters of the cases, there was not even a mention of memory recovery.

Two other highly vocal FMSF Advisory Board members are Dr Elizabeth Loftus and Professor Richard Ofshe. Loftus is a respected academic psychologist whose much-quoted laboratory experiment of successfully implanting a fictitious childhood memory of being lost in a shopping mall is frequently used to defend the false memory syndrome argument. In the experiment, older family members persuaded younger ones of the (supposedly) never real event. However, Loftus herself says that being lost, which almost everyone has experienced, is in no way similar to being abused. Jennifer Freyd comments on the shopping-mall experiment in *Betrayal Trauma* (1996): "If this demonstration proves to hold up under replication it suggests both that therapists can induce false memories and, even more directly, that older family members play a powerful role in defining reality for dependent younger family members" (p. 104).

Elizabeth Loftus herself was sexually abused as a child by a male baby-sitter and admits to blacking the perpetrator out of her memory, although she never forgot the incident. In her autobiography, *Witness for the Defence*, she talks of experiencing flashbacks of this abusive incident on occasion in court in 1985 (Loftus & Ketcham, 1991, p. 149). In her teens, having been told by an uncle that she had found her mother's drowned body, she then started to visualize the scene. Her brother later told her that she had not found the body.

Dr Loftus's successful academic career has run parallel to her even more high-profile career as an expert witness in court, for the defence of those accused of rape, murder, and child abuse. She is described in her own book as the expert who puts memory on trial, sometimes with frightening implications. She used her theories on the unreliability of memory to cast doubt, in 1975, on the testimony of the only eyewitness left alive who could identify Ted Bundy, the all-American boy who was one of America's worst serial rapists and killers (Loftus & Ketcham, 1991, pp. 61–91). Notwithstanding Dr Loftus's arguments, the judge kept Bundy in prison. Bundy was eventually tried, convicted and executed.

Professor Richard Ofshe, Professor of Sociology at Berkeley University, California, is also a high-profile spokesman for the concept of "false memory". Like Elizabeth Loftus, he is an expert witness in court, renowned for having experimentally "implanted" a false memory in the Ingram case to prove that such a thing was possible. Sheriff Paul Ingram admitted abusing his two daughters, when the charges were first put to him in November 1988 by police officers, and before he was interviewed by psychologists. He pleaded guilty and was sentenced in May 1989. Two months later he withdrew his confession and filed to withdraw his guilty pleas. Richard Ofshe's experiment strengthened Ingram's argument that he had been brainwashed into confessing to events which never occurred. This case is often cited by false memory advocates as a classic case of interrogator pressure creating pseudo-memories, although Ingram's wife and other son backed up the central core of the daughters' abuse claims.

In 1990, Appellate Judge Robert H. Peterson reviewed the testimony and evidence of the case. In his summation, he remarked that Ofshe was neither a clinical psychologist, nor an expert in sex abuse. He described Ofshe's implanting experiment as "odd in my judgement" given that Ofshe gave Ingram "a false set of facts, but a set of facts that came pretty close to what one of the victims had accused the defendant of".[3] The judge refused to set aside Ingram's guilty pleas, subsequent appeals have been turned down, and he remains in jail.

Richard Ofshe had been ruled inadmissible as an expert witness in a previous case in which he had appeared for a defendant who claimed that he had committed mail frauds as a result of being "brainwashed" by the Church of Scientology. The court ruling states that Dr Ofshe was not "a mental health professional, his testimony was not relevant to the issue, his theories regarding reform are not generally accepted within the scientific community".[4]

In a more recent case, Ofshe testified for a father accused of abuse by suggesting that the daughter, Lynn Crook, was a victim of "false memory syndrome" implanted by a therapist. The jury rejected his view and found for the daughter, awarding her a large settlement. Judge Yule disliked Ofshe's attitude: "The Court, frankly, found his credibility to be limited by his stridency. . . . It is my experience that heat tends to diminish light . . . unavoidably detracts from his credibility as a thoughtful reasoned expert."[5]

Ofshe's rendering of this case in his book *Making Monsters* (1994), co-authored with Ethan Watters, was criticized in a *Los*

Angeles Times book review: "The tale is an embellished reconstitu-
tion of the court records and discrepancies in the details do not
inspire confidence in Ofshe and Watters' contention that Crook's
memories were caused by reckless therapy and the reading of
self-help books. The authors have fiddled the timeline, making it
appear that Crook read and positively reviewed 'The Courage to
Heal' before, rather than after she recovered memories of abuse"
(Butler, 1995).

Lynn Crook herself, in two long rebuttals of Ofshe's description of her case, said that he "did precisely what he criticized 'bad
therapists' of doing; he modified, omitted and fabricated evidence" (Crook, 1995).

Richard Ofshe is described in his book as a "joint Pulitzer Prize
winner", but recently the Pulitzer Prize Office at Columbia University has been obliged to issue a statement that he does not appear
on any Pulitzer citation.[6]

Others with an interest in promoting the concept of "false
memory" are Paul and Shirley Eberle. They were early advocates,
in the 1980s, of the idea that mothers and mental health professionals fed children stories about sexual abuse. Their first book, *The
Politics of Child Abuse* (1986), made them recognized child abuse
"experts", and they were invited as speakers at conferences for
groups like VOCAL, formed to protect accused parents. Since 1993
their second book, *The Abuse of Innocence*, debunking the famous
nursery-school ritual abuse McMartin case, has been widely cited
by those who claim that cult abuse reports are the result of mass
hysteria.

In fact, the Eberles were hard-core pornographers. In the
1970s, when child pornography laws were less rigid, they edited a
magazine called *Finger* in which there were explicit illustrations of
children involved in sexual acts with adults, as well as scenes of
bondage, S&M, and sexual activities involving urination and def-
ecation. The Eberles themselves are seen in the magazine involved
in sexual acts with each other and with blow-up dolls. One head-
line reads "Wanna Fuck an Editor?" There are also features with
such titles as "Sexpot at Five", "My First Rape, She Was Only
Thirteen", and "Toilet Training".

Another key figure in the false memory syndrome movement
is the New Zealand doctor Felicity Goodyear-Smith. Her book

First Do No Harm (1993) is subtitled *The Sexual Abuse Industry*. It is recommended as "excellent" in the BFMS review, which applauds the author's attempts to downplay what it describes as misplaced professional over-concern about sexual abuse. The reviewer in the BFMS Newsletter, Ivan Tyrrell, says that "her arguments offer a scientific and rational perspective backed by substantial studies and research" in contrast to the hysteria, outrage, and ideological beliefs of the "sexual abuse industry" (Tyrrell, 1994).

In reality, the inaccuracies in the book are legion. The major theme in *First Do No Harm* is that sexual abuse is a cultural taboo, that there is no intrinsic moral objection to adult–child sexual contact and no automatic damage caused by it. Underwager and Wakefield are quoted as the principal reference.

Felicity Goodyear-Smith admits to a personal as well as professional involvement in the abuse field. Her husband and parents-in-law were imprisoned for sexual abuse offences, having been members of a New Zealand community, CentrePoint, that encouraged sexual intimacy amongst its members including the children. In her book, she gives a highly equivocal account of a situation in which under-age girls were encouraged to have *public sex* with her father-in-law, and on occasion, she says, her mother-in-law took part as well "in threesome situations". Both were given terms in prison for those offences.

Instead of condemning outright what were sexually perverse and damaging practices on the part of those adults who were convicted, she says that the more "independent" girls "initiated" the encounters. Nowhere does Goodyear-Smith attribute responsibility for the sexual malpractices to the adults, who failed to maintain proper boundaries and who used under-age girls to meet their sexual needs. "Inappropriate" is the strongest comment she makes. She also says, quite staggeringly in the circumstances, "it seems clear that the subsequent counselling and legal intervention they have undergone may have contributed to their seeing themselves as seriously and permanently harmed from their *childhood sexual experimentation*" (my emphasis).

She questions whether the memories could possibly be accurate and reliable about what happened "so long ago" (just over ten years). She also queries the motives of those who persuaded the young adult women to bring the charges.

Goodyear-Smith quotes studies that purport to show that adult–child sex can be harmless. Under a section on "Children's Sexual Rights", she describes groups such as the Paedophile Information Exchange, the Rene Guyon Society ("sex by eight, or it's too late"), and the North American Man/Boy Love Association as "holding *radical* [my emphasis] beliefs regarding children's sexual rights". She further says: "As would be expected, these societies have mostly been disbanded or outlawed in the *sexually repressive* [my emphasis] 1980s and 1990s."

The studies that Goodyear-Smith quoted are by Theo Sandfort and M. Baurmann. Sandfort was a board member of *Paedika*, the Dutch paedophile magazine, and his study consisted of interviewing twenty-five boys who had been recruited by their current adult lovers through a Netherlands paedophile network (Sandfort, 1983). They "demonstrated", to Sandfort's satisfaction, that sexual friendships between men and boys produced no evidence of harm! The Baurmann study is presented as assessing 8,058 young people and finding that not one of the 1,000 boys under 14 was found to be harmed. In fact, only 112 young people were sampled for symptoms; of those, only 13 were boys, and they tended to be victims of less serious and extra-familial abuse (Baurmann, 1983).

The age of sexual consent, Goodyear-Smith thinks, is unenforceable and should be removed from the statute books (this would, of course, be a paedophile's Charter).

She highlights famous child-abuse cases that have not resulted in convictions, suggesting that they were completed unfounded, even though a more thorough appraisal of the detail of many of these cases reveals information that is highly consistent with real sexual abuse. She even questions sexual abuse cases that led to conviction, such as the Christchurch Civic Day Care case. On appeal, the New Zealand court concluded that there was no basis for the claims that evidence of children had been contaminated by interviewing techniques or by parental hysteria. The court had no misgivings about the outcome, and the convictions stood. Goodyear-Smith emphasizes that the allegations of child abuse in the Australian Children of God sect were unfounded.

Like Goodyear-Smith, the BFMS is also espousing the cause of the Children of God, to an extent that has caused the resignation of one of its Advisory Board Member. Dr Elizabeth Tylden, Honorary

Consultant Psychiatrist, UCH and Middlesex Hospital Medical School, resigned as member of the BFMS Advisory Board early in 1995. She said (personal communication): "I became aware that the FMS were actively supporting 'The Family', formerly Children of God. I have experience of gross sexual impropriety to which children in this organization have been exposed. Roger Scotford (the chairman) wrote to me after I had resigned saying he was going to support cult members who had been falsely accused."

Dr Tylden is a respected expert on cults, and she had recognized two of the British "Children of God" leaders at a conference in London at which Dr Paul McHugh, FMSF Advisory Board member, was a featured speaker. The two cult leaders, Gideon and Rachel Scott, were registered under Roger Scotford's home address, along with the other twenty-six BFMS delegates.

An *Observer* newspaper survey on cults wrote:

> It is difficult to find a cult with a worse reputation than the Children of God (now known as the Family). As recently as October of last year a teenage girl was awarded £5000 by the British Criminal Injuries Compensation Board having been abused by members of the sect from the age of 3. It is estimated that of the 9000 current members of The Family, 6,000 are children; many of them the offspring of the sect's "Hookers for Christ" campaign in the 1970s and 1980s in which women members seduced potential converts and bore their children. . . . Members were urged to "share" each other's wives and husbands, pornography was circulated, sex with children was elliptically condoned and "God's Whores" were instructed to pick up men in discos and bars. [*Observer*, 14 May 1995, Life, p. 6]

Linda Berg, daughter of the cult's founder David Berg who died in 1994, has spoken publicly about her "evil father" and of sexual abuse in the cult, which has spread through the United States, South America, Europe, India, and Australasia (*Daily Mail*, 31 October 1994).

Another hotly argued "recovered memory case" was the retrial of George Franklin in California, who in 1990 was given life after his daughter, Eileen, recovered what she believed to be a 21-year-old memory of him raping and murdering her schoolfriend. Although proponents of "false memory" argue that this is not possible, Eileen Franklin produced details of evidence which matched police files and which her attorney argued she could not have known about other than by being there. Her father was a violent alcoholic who regularly beat the family. When he was arrested, the police found that his tiny Sacramento apartment was filled to the brim with child-sized dildos, child pornography, and books on incest (Terr, 1994). The prosecution in 1990 filed documents that he had sexually assaulted his daughters and other young girls, and had a fascination for deviant sexual practices between humans and animals. They listed twelve pages of pornographic materials, some involving himself, found in his possession.[7]

* * *

This has been an exceptionally difficult, dirty public debate—though less so in the United Kingdom, which is not as litigious as the United States. Holding to a position that allows for the complexities and uncertainties of traumatic memory has not been easy. Keeping a sense of perspective about the false allegations which do unhappily sometimes occur, and trying to impress an undereducated media and public about the widespread occurrence of false denials on the part of child abusers, has been even more of an uphill struggle.

While bad practice must clearly be vigorously eliminated, good practice must be just as vigorously defended. The major psychiatric, psychological, and psychotherapy organizations have been slow in finding a voice and have dismally failed to stand up for the corpus of knowledge which is or should be their preserve. They have allowed themselves to be damaged by their non-response to the "false memory" argument. In not defending themselves, they have put their adult abuse patients more at risk and contributed to a situation in which abused children are more vulnerable to being disbelieved. The one honourable exception is the British Psychological Society, whose report on recovered memories was the best of its kind to date amongst the world organizations and is much to be applauded, but it is only a beginning. There needs to be much more.

Accuracy about Abuse (AAA) was formed in early 1994 with the primary aim of stemming the flow of misinformation in the media about "false memory syndrome", which it was believed would have damaging consequences for abused children in court and for adult survivors seeking treatment.

Backed by MIND, AAA was set up as an information network-ing system to inform media, legal, and political circles of the latest sexual abuse research and to provide the background to badly reported media controversies. Initially, the concentration was on material gained from adult therapy, though it has always been the intention to broaden the scope of the information sheets to include material more specific to children. It has grown in four years to an international mailing-list membership of over 1,000, mainly or-ganizations, social work departments, therapy groups, lawyers, academic researchers, rape and incest crisis groups, and survivor groups. The networking of information is working particularly well at a national and international level. It has an outreach of considerably in excess of 10,000.

Clearly, parents who are falsely accused of sexual abuse need backing. It is in no one's interests that, in the interests of promoting justice for the many, justice is forgotten for the few. Arguments about whether the protection of innocent children has a higher status than the protection of innocent adults get society nowhere. Neither position is acceptable. Protection for the few innocent par-ents who are falsely accused will come from a higher awareness of child abuse out in society at large and a consequent increase in prosecution and conviction rates. Where false denials are allowed to stand for the truth, then genuine denials have no real chance of being heard.

NOTES

1. *Underwager and Wakefield v. Salter et al.*, No. 93-2422, W.D. Wisconsin, 1994.

2. Freyd, W. Letter to WGBH-Boston, dated 17 April 1995.

3. Peterson, R. H.., *State of Washington v. Paul Ross Ingram*, Superior Court of the State of Washington in and for the County of Thurston, Proceedings, Vol. VII, No. 88-1-752-1, 1990.

4. *USA v. Fishman*, No. CR-88-0616-DL, U.S. District Court for Northern District of California, 13 April 1990.

5. *Crook v. Murphy*, Case No. 91-2-0011-2-5. Before the Honorable Dennis D. Yule, Superior Court Judge. Benton, State of Washington, 4 March 1994.

6. Letter: The Pulitzer Prize, Office of the Administrator, 1 May 1996.

7. C-24395, a Memorandum of Points and Authorities re: admissibility of evidence pursuant to evidence code section 2201(B). *People of the State of California v. George Thomas Franklin, Snr.*, Superior Court of the State of California in and for the Court of San Mateo, 11 October 1990.

CHAPTER EIGHT

Serving two masters:
a patient, a therapist,
and an allegation of sexual abuse

Leslie Ironside

In this chapter, Leslie Ironside analyses a painful situation with which therapists are having to deal; when an abused child anticipates abuse in the therapy or distorts what is happening because he or she views all events through the prism of traumatic knowledge. Without polarizing or blaming, Leslie Ironside uses his training and experience to trace compassionately how such situations can arise.

"We don't see things as they are, we see them as we are."

Anaïs Nin

"It's often safer to be in chains than to be free."

Franz Kafka

Therapists frequently have to struggle with the question of the veracity of what they are being told and to bear witness to the difficulties that patients might have as they, too, struggle with the question of the validity of their own memories. It is, though, important that therapists bear in mind the difference between patients' attempts to relate an event truthfully—that is,

the struggle with memory—from the separate issue of what patients might want therapists to believe—that is, how patients
might consciously or unconsciously alter what is communicated
according to the present situation.

This issue takes on a particularly concrete dimension if a patient makes a false allegation of abuse, as a real, mutually
witnessed event is transposed in the patient's mind to something
quite different, and, at that point in time, the patient is clearly
communicating a wish for something other than the actual experience to be believed. Such an event leads to important questions as
regards the role of the therapist: how a therapist might be seen as
an abuser, how this relates to the actual experience in the consulting-room and in the patient's life history, and what light this might
throw on a patient's pathology.

In his paper "Observations on Transference-Love", Freud discussed the difficult technical issues of a patient falling in love with
an analyst and the implications for technique and the strains that
this can place upon the analytic relationship (Freud, 1915a). He
concluded with the powerful thought that the therapeutic aim of
psychoanalysis was "to handle the most dangerous mental impulses and to obtain mastery over them for the sake of the patient"
(p. 171).

Bion (1959, 1962b) later developed the concept of container and
contained to describe the early infantile relationship between a
mother and her child. Segal (1981) clearly summarizes how in this
model

> the infant's relation to his first object can be described as fol-
> lows: when an infant has an intolerable anxiety, he deals with
> it by projecting it into his mother. The mother's response is to
> acknowledge the anxiety and do whatever is necessary to re-
> lieve the infant's distress. The infant's perception is that he has
> projected something intolerable into his object, but the object
> was capable of containing it and dealing with it. He can then
> reintroject not only his original anxiety but an anxiety modi-
> fied by having been contained. He also introjects an object
> capable of containing and dealing with anxiety.

This concept of container and contained, and Winnicott's (1960)
subtly different concept of "holding", are often also used to describe metaphorically psychotherapists' relationship to their

patients and clearly link with Freud's dictum of obtaining mastery over dangerous mental impulses.

The situation involving a false allegation of sexual abuse by a therapist is a most testing example of attempting to contain (Bion), hold (Winnicott), or obtain mastery over (Freud) "dangerous mental impulses" and raises crucial questions as regards the nature of memory and the relationship and difference between an individual's memory and what might best be described as the purpose of any particular communication.

In this chapter, I describe and explore what I have learnt from an experience with one particular child, Jim, in which an allegation led to a full diagnostic interview, a temporary breakdown in therapy, and, finally, a return to therapy. First, however, I would like to place this experience within a wider context through the exploration of work with three other patients in which allegations of various sorts were made but which did not lead to a belief within the professional network that there was any substance to them. In these three cases, the presenting material could then be thought through within the clinical setting and an attempt could be made to understand and "obtain mastery" of (Freud) the material. This contrasts with the fourth case, which resulted in diagnostic interviews and a break in therapy—the correct course of action at that point, but one that served to mask rather than address the child's pathology.

Patient A: John

John was 13 at the time of referral but had the stature of a child many years his junior. One year prior to the referral, he had made an allegation that he had been abducted by a man and a woman and forced to have intercourse with the woman. No prosecution was ever made. A considerable amount of help had been offered to him and his family through the local family centre, and at the point of referral to me he was no longer in the house-bound state that he had been in for much of the previous year. At the initial meetings, he refused to see me alone, and so his mother remained in the room. He spoke of how he felt that he no longer trusted anybody except his family, and it soon transpired that there had been a long history of bullying and many difficulties in terms of separation prior to the alleged incident. Gradually, John settled enough to allow his mother to stay in the waiting-room, which was very close to the consulting-room, but both doors had to remain open. Unfortunately, during the first of the sessions when I was alone with him, he heard voices from another part of the building. John immediately become very anxious, and I, in a way that with hindsight might seem insensitive, asked if it would be helpful to shut the door. He now became overtly quite overwhelmed and tearful and wanted his mother. I asked his mother to come in.

Discussion

In his *Brazilian Lectures* (1990), Bion describes how in "every consulting room there ought to be two rather frightened people: the patient and the psycho-analyst" (p. 5), but I think that John's fears go one step further than this. When his mother came back into the consulting-room after the incident described, John was able to think about and discuss his fear; he also described how the voices had reminded him of the abductors and of how my then suggesting that the door should be closed linked me immediately with the gang and left him petrified and, of importance, of course, cut off from his mother. This immediately conjures up a picture of the need to consider complex emotional factors related to the infantile and primitive, as well as the present precipitating trauma. We can see from this example how in these perhaps extreme circumstances a patient can quickly see the therapist as an abuser. At the point of my suggesting shutting the door, John no longer seemed able to think symbolically—I seemed concretely, in Segal's terms, to become one of the abusing gang (Segal, 1991).

Patient B: Tony

Tony was 8 years old at the point of referral. Adshead (1994), in her review of the literature on false allegations of sexual abuse in childhood, states that in 96 per cent of such cases children do not deliberately set out to make trouble for adults. This did not seem to be the case with Tony, a boy who was causing immense anxiety to the professional network. His history was appalling. Both his parents had died of drug overdoses, Tony himself discovering his mother's dead body one morning. His early childhood is likely to have been a haze of confusing images and awful events. He found it very difficult to relate to people—many would, of course, empathize with his story, but his coldness and violent behaviour would inevitably lead to a fiercely negative spiral of interaction. At the point of referral, there were immense concerns as regards his behaviour, a sense that he had never mourned for his parents and that he was finding it difficult to form meaningful relationships.

His attitude to therapy was, needless to say, very ambivalent, and I often felt that he would do all within his power to try to end the sessions. The professional network, though, remained steadfast in its opinion that Tony should continue in therapy. This was very difficult, and it was only due to immense effort and close communication between all the professionals involved that we managed to survive his attacks upon any commitment to form a therapeutic alliance with me and consequently to struggle with the dependency feelings that this would entail. I purposefully say "we", as it was very much a group effort, with the escort who brought Tony being a very key figure in what was eventually felt to be a successful outcome to therapy.

The attacks were very forceful, going to the extent of his bruising himself and then making accusations that I had hit him. At times, I had to restrain him in the room, and, at times, the escort had to carry him physically into the room. He was also verbally very aggressive, though it was not so much what he said but the force with which he said things that made it so difficult to relate to him. He also said that he was going to tell his social worker that I had sexually abused him and then I would be locked up.

We always approached his behaviour as a communication of a frame of mind that needed to be understood, rather than to be acted upon in the sense of ending the sessions or formally investigating the allegations. This began to pay dividends, as I think he began to feel that his internal rage could be understood. It was, however, very difficult to maintain this frame of mind and not to feel overwhelmed by the thought that we were just cruelly and sadistically punishing him further. Then, in one particular session, Tony greatly enlightened me, and his actions gave me the courage to continue the work. During the session, I had to deal with the most difficult attacks, both verbal and physical. Towards the end, he said that he was going to write me a letter. He had recently taken to writing, and, although this activity was often loaded with insults, I had seen it as a positive development in itself. (Interestingly, this coincided with the beginnings of some progress in his written work at school.) He quickly and secretly wrote something which he took with him and posted back through the letter box after the session ended. I had expected something similar to his other writings—"Fuck off Ironside. I hate you"—but what he had written was: "Dear Ironside . . . I like you really . . . Tony." Needless to say, this greatly reinforced the importance of continuing the sessions despite the part of Tony that acted as a powerful saboteur, almost destroying any hope of forming a close relationship and, I feel, giving a particularly dramatic exposition of the saying, "He is his own worst enemy".

Gradually, Tony allowed his foster-parents to form a closer relationship with him, both physically and emotionally, and, again gradually, he began to form a more caring relationship with me in which he began to relate his life history, without re-traumatization.

Discussion

In the article "Love and Death in the Transference: The Case of the Hungarian Poet Attila Jozsef", the author Mauro Mancia (1993) describes the equally powerful negative transference between Jozsef and his analyst which, as with Tony, was likely to have its origins in his infantile experience. Of most relevance to the theme of this chapter, however, are the following free associations, which he communicated in the form of blank verse.

> I'll try lying ...
> I'll mix truth with lies, I won't take it lying down ...
> so I'll screw her up in her everyday life, outside analysis
> I'll ruin her in her profession
> I'll pass the word "by chance" that I've had it off with her ...
> that way I'll get her to lick my arse
> that was the relationship my mother got me into with her
> behaviour ...

This was written in 1936 just prior to his breaking off analysis. In December 1937, Attila Jozsef committed suicide at the age of 32, throwing himself under a train.

The subject, then, of false allegations of this malicious type is thus not a new one, although I think that the difference today is that such allegations can be thought about when working with a child of the tender age of 6 years who might or might not himself have been sexually abused. As in the case of Attila Jozsef and his awful death, my experience with Tony seemed also to indicate a very troubled person. He related to the outside world according to an internal phantasy of the "everybody is my enemy" kind. Generally, his relationships were governed by a state of projective identification (Klein, 1946), dominated by a way of relating not with a person as separate from himself, with their own thoughts and feelings, but with this image projected into another person and then related to as though it belonged to that other person. The mechanism of projective identification has both developmental and defensive potential but this was a very rigid defensive position with the consequent confusion of ego boundaries and the formation of a relationship based on part objects that took a great deal of time to work through with Tony. He was referred in the first place because of concerns as regards the mourning process, and, as John Steiner (1993) argues in *Psychic Retreats*, it is in the process of mourning that the deep-rooted issues involved in projective identification can be resolved.

Without entering into the debate as to how one measures successful therapeutic outcome (cf. Boston & Lush, 1994), there was a general consensus in the network that Tony benefited a great deal from therapy. The key factor in this success seemed to be the close cooperation and mutual support that existed within that network. It was a system that was able to bear the allegations and remained convinced that these were manifestations of psychic distress and not matters that needed to be acted upon, other than ensuring that there was supportive professional contact at all times and an overt recognition of the destructive way in which Tony could relate. This theme of the importance of good communication within the professional network and awareness of processes such as destructive splitting is something that is so often stressed in the literature—for example, Reder and Duncan (1993), Bentovim (1992), and Sinason (1994).

Patient C: Peter

Peter was referred because of unmanageable behaviour that was beginning to threaten seriously his adoptive placement. He was a boy who had been multiply abused prior to his being taken into care, and he brought to therapy all the vexed issues associated with working with children who have been abused (cf. Boston & Szur, 1983; Szur & Miller, 1992). Again, there was within the professional network the very close communication that is so necessary in this type of work. Peter would be very flamboyant in his acting out and, in a tragicomic way, would call out the window that I was sexually abusing him, telling his escort and his social worker a similar story.

Discussion

On a conscious level he was alleging abuse, but in a way that meant that the allegations would not be taken seriously. This way of relating did give me, as the therapist, some insight into his internal world and into the relationships of his internal objects, but I would like to concentrate here on the issue of the allegations, which were not viewed by the network as warranting an investigation of the immediate events but, rather, were taken seriously and seen as a communication of a frame of mind that was particularly relevant in terms of this boy's life history.

This way of behaving must also be viewed in a wider context, in that this kind of behaviour, like the humourless behaviour exemplified by Tony, may be exhibited by children who have not been abused. Colleagues in both social work and teaching speak of observing this behaviour both with their own children professionally and with a wide spectrum of children not confined to those in which there is suggestion of abuse. The knowledge of child sexual abuse is now abroad in the playground. This is the negative side of the more positive movement to raise public awareness and is an area of great concern at present, as professionals struggle to deal with the malicious allegations of abuse whilst recognizing that professional abuse does occur. There are side-effects to increased public awareness of sexual abuse, one of which is how the conscious and unconscious anxieties brought about through such knowledge are borne both by children and by adults.

Allegation and investigation:
Patient D

In contrast to the above three patients, Patient D made an allegation that was felt to warrant a full investigation. This experience highlights the struggle to ensure that a child is being adequately protected—professional abuse does take place—while paying attention to the very damaging impact of a false accusation upon a professional, and, indeed, upon the course of a child's therapy.

Jim, a 4-year-old who had been multiply abused, including incidents of brutal sexual abuse, made an allegation to his foster-mother, following the first session after an Easter break, that I had given him some medication that had made him sleepy and that I had then "played" with his penis. It was an allegation that had to be pursued in terms of child protection; a case conference was held, and a full diagnostic interview involving the police and social workers was completed. As a result of this allegation, not only was Jim's own therapy threatened but my own professional and personal life was placed under scrutiny and threat.

As Attila Jozsef wrote:

> so I'll screw her up in her everyday life, outside analysis
> I'll ruin her in her profession.

Such an issue blurs the boundary between the personal and professional life of the therapist.

The context

I saw Jim once weekly in my consulting-room at home. This is a situation that must rank high in terms of (1) the possibility of an allegation being made, because of such a child's heightened feelings of vulnerability at being alone with an adult, and (2) providing a context that could be a high-risk one for such an allegation being believed and acted upon within the professional network rather than being seen as a transference manifestation. The fact that I am a male worker, though Jim had been abused by his mother and possibly by other adults, placed me in a vulnerable position in terms of working with sexual abuse, because such abuse is so readily associated with the notion of the male perpetrator. In addition, the fact that I was not seeing him in a clinic setting, with, for instance, colleagues in the next room, served to heighten the issue in terms of containing professional anxiety within the network.

Jim was seen in the same context as the three patients I have described, but with different professional personnel involved, and a great deal of time and effort was spent in endeavouring to ensure that there was a sound working relationship within the professional network. There was, however, something fundamentally different about this experience which, I believe, goes further than that being explicable in terms of these different professional people and which serves to illuminate a part of the child's pathology.

The referral and early therapy

I have not met his mother, but I think that it is of immense importance to understand something of her history and frame of mind in order to understand Jim. Reports describe how she appeared to have been badly abused—physically, emotionally, and sexually—by her own parents. Additionally, she was perceived as being fundamentally disturbed by this abuse and seemed to repeat the damaging behaviour in her adult life. The extent of her disturbance was reflected in her confusion between her dreams, fantasies, and memories. She had apparently spoken to her social worker of having sex in the back of a car with her father, of bad dreams of her brother getting into bed with her, and of masturbating while imagining that her father was doing this. In all these conversations, she was not clear whether they were dreams or actual recollections.

When Jim was referred to therapy he was no longer living with his mother, but there were immense concerns regarding his behaviour. He could be very withdrawn but at other times would explode with immense anger. He could not be trusted to be left alone with animals or younger children and had been found with his finger in the anus of a dog, and he seemed very preoccupied with children's bottoms and vaginas. He had also been known to self-mutilate, severely scratching his own face and groin.

At the start of therapy, it was very difficult to see him alone. He seemed overwhelmed by anxiety at the thought of his foster-mother leaving the room. Gradual interpretation of both the separation anxiety and the fear of being alone with me led to independent sessions. In some of these sessions, he would often explore quite sexualized material and seemed to show anxiety that I would want to abuse him or enter some kind of sexualized relationship with him.

Jim did exhibit sexualized behaviour in the room and did at times remove his clothes. Sometimes he also wet his clothes by urinating in them, but also through his play with the water. I kept a spare set of clothes for him. This was all known within the professional framework.

At times, his behaviour was also very puzzling and anxiety-provoking to me, a fact that had led me to seek consultation on the case with an experienced, senior colleague. The session after which he made his accusation had itself been discussed in depth in consultation; interestingly, the session had been marked by the complete absence of the previous behaviour that had caused so much concern. This was commented on within the consultation prior to my being aware of the allegation.

The arrangement for consultation was made before the session with Jim, and the session was therefore written-up carefully. It was not the sort of session that I might normally have thought of recording in detail or of discussing within the professional network. I hold a model of professional confidentiality where, if there are particular sessions in which a child exhibits behaviour that could easily be subject to misrepresentation, I ensure that this is well recorded and that the general and—if need be—particular points of concern are known to the appropriate professional colleagues. It is important to distinguish between confidentiality and secrecy, especially as the latter is such an issue for abused children.

I had been meeting with Jim for some nine months prior to the break forced by the allegation. During this time I had built up a good working partnership with the professional network, including the foster-parents. This partnership seemed open, and we had discussed the difficulties that they were experiencing, including the foster-mother's fears that Jim might make some allegation against her or her partner. The professional network was also aware of the struggle that this presented for me as a therapist working with Jim, but the consensus was that it was important to maintain therapy and to endeavour to work through these issues.

The allegation

I think it might be useful to relate the events as they occurred, as they are illustrative of some of the difficulties that colleagues might experience in similar cases. Jim had returned to therapy after the Easter break. The following week I was informed by the foster-mother that he was not well, though I had also been informed that he had begun at a play group and it did seem odd that he was well enough to attend that. The next week I was given similar information, and I spoke to the key social worker, saying that I felt that things did not add up and was wondering what was happening. He confirmed that Jim was not well. This continued for three weeks, with my sensing that there was something strange going on but being unable to put my finger on quite what it was. There was then a telephone call from the police saying that they wanted to talk to me. I presumed that this was over another case in which, interestingly, there were strong suggestions of professional abuse by a child care worker. When I managed to speak to the police officer, he mentioned that he wanted to speak to me regarding Jim but could not at this point divulge why. We arranged a meeting, my presumption now being that perhaps there were further court cases regarding his earlier life history prior to being accepted into care and that the police were wanting an opinion. I was left perplexed as to why the social worker had not spoken to me of this but was unable to get further clarification. When the police officers met with me, they began by endeavouring to make it clear that they were meeting with me to seek information rather than interviewing a suspect for an offence. They then described how Jim had told the social worker that I had interfered with him. I was informed that a case conference had been held and a diagnostic interview. Though I was very shocked, I was also relieved that I could now make sense of my recent experience.

The police seemed very conversant with issues of child abuse and with the concept of transference and were very sensitive and supportive. Their report said that they felt that there was no substance to the allegations and that Jim should resume therapy as soon as possible. When I contacted the social workers, concerned to clarify matters, I was given the following information. After the session Jim had told his foster-mother that I had removed his trousers and played with his penis and that I had also given him some red medication to make him go to sleep. She had then discussed this with the foster-agency social worker who had quite rightly taken it up with the social services department (SSD) that referred Jim, with the SSD where he lives, and with the social workers where I live. The network in this case was very complicated and involved a private fostering agency, three SSDs, and two police authorities. A decision was made to hold a diagnostic interview, in

which Jim firmly repeated the allegations. The team of social workers and police felt that it was a transference issue but decided that
the police should complete their own investigations. A number of
people had by this time been informed of the allegation and of the
measures that were being taken—all, of course, unknown to me.
The case conference decision was that Jim was not to return to
therapy until the police investigation had been completed. There
seemed to be some hiccup in the procedure as it took several
weeks for the investigation to be completed. My own opinion is
that some time limit should have been placed on procedures at this
first meeting and a second case conference held to close the matter.
After the police met with me, the SSD did not seem to feel that it
was their responsibility to hold a further case conference. I was
told by the team manager that they viewed their brief as that of
child protection in a limited sense of safety and physical protection
and "had moved on to the next case". It was very much left to me
to ensure that my name was cleared and for me and the agency
social worker to try to plan for Jim's return to therapy. This
seemed to reflect a poor balance between a quite rigid child-protection brief and the more complex issues of the impact of this
experience upon the child and upon the credibility of the professional involved.

After an inexplicably long period of time and pressure from me
that this matter should be formally closed, the police in the child's
area of residence eventually wrote a note saying that I had been
interviewed and it was decided that no further action would be
taken in respect of the matter. This was clearly an inadequate
document in terms of my needs as it placed me in the same category as someone with whom there was strong suspicion but lack
of firm evidence. Given that the SSD would not hold a formal case
conference, a planning meeting had to be held, attended by my
local SSD representative together with the investigating police and
the agency social worker. Apologies for non-attendance were sent
from the other two SSDs. I had also had discussion with my professional association, the Association of Child Psychotherapists,
which it was very useful to call upon as an external authority. The
police officer again made clear his position and was in full agreement that the note written by his colleague in the other police

department was inadequate. He allowed his earlier report, which detailed matters more coherently, to be circulated to all parties. It all highlighted the inadequacy of procedures, in that I had to provide the impetus to ensure that all parties who had been told of the alleged abuse were also informed that there was absolutely no substance to the allegations.

Although it had only been my work with Jim that had been interrupted, my local SSD now recommended that I be allowed to continue to meet with children and supervise staff, and I was given clearance that I was not seen to be a danger to my own children! Such is the manner in which such an investigation can invade one's professional and personal life.

Impact upon the therapist

Situations like this place an inevitable strain on all the professionals involved as they erode the very fabric of open, mutually supportive, and trusting professional relationships. They place, however, a particular—if obvious—strain upon the alleged abuser as she or he has to struggle with a very disturbing awareness of being seen in such a light. I certainly found the experience extremely stressful and feel very fortunate in having a very supportive wife and family as well as supportive friends and colleagues. I think that it is vital to acknowledge that, if such an allegation were to be made when the alleged abuser was, for whatever reason, already in a vulnerable state, the consequences could be quite catastrophic. When I was first informed of the allegation, I was left feeling very angry, not so much with Jim but at the way in which the matter had been handled. I was also aware of a feeling that might well have arisen however it had been managed: an internal voice of incredulity that my integrity had been in some way doubted. This I had to try simultaneously to reconcile with an awareness of the necessity for correct child-protection procedures. I was also very anxious about the other children whom I saw in therapy, and even now, some considerable time after the incident, I feel concerned that if further allegations are made by other children, they will be linked to this incident and I will, as a consequence, be treated with added suspicion. I fear that there is no way that one's name can be completely cleared once such an allegation has been made.

That the allegation also led to a statement as regards my relationship to my own children filled me with a deeper despair. This sentence really brought the matter home to me. I then realized with a vengeance that there had been the possibility of further and very distressing consequences to my personal life and that of my family. They could have been completely shattered. I had become increasingly furious at how uncontained things had felt and at how difficult it had proved to ensure that whoever had been told of the allegation was also informed that my name had been cleared. This latest statement—"not a danger to my own children", which meant that prior to that it was considered as a possibility— really underlined the point. I do not think that the serious impact of the allegation of abuse upon myself as the alleged abuser was adequately borne in mind by the child-protection officers. This experience really highlighted for me the very real danger that, if such matters are not thoroughly considered and—of utmost importance—"contained", they become in themselves a form of professional abuse.

Understandably, I felt very cautious about resuming work with Jim. I stood to lose a great deal, and before taking him back into therapy I had to ensure that an appropriate framework existed in case there were any future allegations.

Planning the return to therapy

Through a range of discussions with various colleagues I arrived at the following proposal.

1. If it was possible, as it was important for Jim's development, therapy should be resumed, but there was no reason to presume that there would not be repeated allegations in the future.

2. Future sessions would be tape-recorded as a way of balancing child-protection issues and the need to protect myself. This would, in a way, play into the very pathology that I was trying

to work through, but it seemed unavoidable in terms of protecting my professional credibility.

3.   Following audio-taping, a senior colleague would, if any fur-
     ther allegations were made, be able to listen to the recordings
     and act as an "incident assessor" and to avoid a repeat of the
     break in therapy and the difficult diagnostic procedure that had
     been experienced—unless this were to prove absolutely neces-
     sary.

There are, of course, recognizable shortcomings in using this
proposal as a safety net, but I feel that some of these are inevitable
as one is seeking a procedural solution to a psychological problem.
There was, for instance, some pressure to install video facilities,
but what happens with a child who is too young or too frightened
to go to the toilet alone? Does one also install a camera in the toilet,
or can one only do this work if a colleague is permanently available to cover any eventuality?

Comment

In Freud's paper on "transference-love" (1915a), he makes the very
important distinction between "acting out" and "remembering"
and sees them as opposite and antithetical paths for bringing the
past into the present. "Acting out" is seen to occur in the motor
sphere of action, remembering in the "psychical sphere" of
mentalization and verbalization. "Acting out" remains faithful to
its origins and does not undergo the same transforming process of
reconstruction that a memory inevitably does. In discussing
"transference-love", Freud describes how "if the patient's ad-
vances were returned . . . she would have succeeded . . . in acting
out, in repeating in real life, what she ought only to have remembered, to have reproduced as psychical material and to have kept
within the sphere of psychical events" (p. 166).
     Searle (1969), in the development of "speech–act" theory, use-
fully shows how in certain verbal expressions this distinction is not
clear. Some statements—such as "I declare the Olympics Open"—

are performative, and some specific acts can only be performed in words. These are acts in the guise of psychical expressions (Stern, 1993). The expression "X has alleged that Y abused him" carries with it, in certain circumstances, this sense of action within the words and, as such, is a statement that can of itself lead to a radical, and irretrievable, change in a relationship.

With Jim, the decision to hold a case conference and to stop therapy blurred the distinction between "acting out" and "remembering". The experience of an allegation being made, and acted upon, then placed the key figures in the system—child, therapist, social worker, foster-parent, and so on—in a very different state from what they were in before. It was important not only to recognize the conscious difficulties that might arise from this, but also to pay due attention to the unconscious processes that might influence and subvert the way in which the situation was managed. In these circumstances, the key figures become organized in a way more akin to what Bentovim (1992) describes as a "trauma-organized system", and, if resources are available, it would be useful to engage an external consultant formally at this point. The impact on the child, the therapist, and the relationship between them is likely to be extreme, as, too, is that between the therapist and the professional network. The social worker and foster-mother had, for example, been forced to entertain the idea that I, as a colleague whom they trusted and to whom they had sent a child in their care, might also be an abuser. In consequence, they had both felt obliged to lie to me. I, for my part, had to struggle with being seen in this light and being lied to.

Working with any child that has been multiply abused places immense strain upon the therapist and the professional network. There is a constant pressure to enact with the patient his or her perverse internal object relationships. In this case, thinking about the network as a whole, the correct decision to hold a diagnostic interview meant that the team moved from the "psychical sphere" and treated this as an experience that might have happened. This has very important repercussions in terms of the child's therapy and whether or not it can be resumed, as it raises the related questions as to whether the relationships between the child and the therapist and between the therapist and the professional network have been irretrievably changed, and, if so, whether they have changed in a way that makes it impossible to continue therapy.

As a team, and after considerable discussion, we decided to continue Jim's therapy. Obviously, the experience was felt to have had an impact upon the relationship between Jim and me, and between the network and me, but this was not felt to be irretrievable. I looked forward—with interest but also undoubted apprehension—to resuming therapy with Jim and to exploring this dynamic in the consulting-room.

Jane Milton (1994) describes how hard it is to strike the right balance when working with victims of abuse:

> Sympathetic attention to the person who has been a helpless victim is essential. At the same time it is vital to address what is perhaps the most serious aspect of the victim's plight: her corruption in childhood via excessive stimulation of her own hatred and destructiveness, which becomes eroticized, and her identification with the aggressor, often as a means of psychic survival. [p. 243]

Jim had been badly abused as a child, and it was, of course, important to pay sympathetic attention to this; at the same time it was vital to keep in mind the corruption that had occurred in his childhood and the possible identification with the aggressor. Much of my apprehension as regards resuming therapy with Jim rested upon my experience as a "helpless victim" within a situation brought about through his actions.

Return to therapy

We had decided that it would be best to have a meeting between the social worker, the foster-mother, Jim, and me in order to go through what had happened and to offer Jim some explanation as regards continuing therapy and the safeguards that we had decided to implement—most importantly, the use of a tape-recorder in the sessions. At this session, Jim arrived "full of beans", quickly settling to his toys and behaving in a quite jovial way. He played separately from the adult group, and we, as a group, felt it impor-

tant for him to come over and to listen to what was being discussed. The events were run over, and Jim was asked to contribute
to this. The whole tone of the session then became quite different
and very sober. Jim was silent when asked to recount the events,
and his foster-mother struggled to encourage him to relate what
had happened and what he had told her. This part of the session
felt very uncomfortable and persecutory, but, as Jim and his foster-
mother related the events, I could quite see how the allegation was
taken seriously. Importantly, in terms of the countertransference
this whole procedure felt quite unreal, as I struggled to listen to
what was being related and process this alongside my own
memory of the session.

The social worker explained how important returning to
therapy was and that the sessions would be recorded so that, in the
future, if Jim felt after a session that I had done something, he
could again tell his foster-mother and the tape could then be listened to, to see if he had confused his memory of the sessions and
what actually happened. This would protect him and me from
further police investigations, unless they were felt to be absolutely
necessary.

This part of the session was then drawn to a close, and the
social worker and the foster-mother left. The tone of things had
gradually grown more light-hearted, and Jim spoke of feeling ok at
being left alone with me.

This encounter was obviously very different from the normal
events of long-term work with a child. I felt that procedurally it
was necessary if therapy was to continue, but it felt bizarre and
confusing. It was important to bear in mind during the meeting
that Jim had been through a number of investigative interviews,
the impact of which would have been different from those of the
primary trauma. The role of the investigator—establishing what
had happened—was clearly different from that of the therapist,
and the role of the child in a diagnostic interview was likewise
different. This meeting was attempting to bridge that gap.

I was certainly working in an atmosphere beyond my experience as a child psychotherapist, but the disassociation that I
experienced between my memory of the session and how it was
being recounted by Jim, and the split between his light-hearted/

jovial and sombre/persecuted state, also reminded me that in cases of childhood sexual abuse the victim can enter into a disassociated state as a result of the trauma (Putnam, 1985).

The whole issue of the use of the tape recorder also meant that there was still a certain amount of necessary "acting out" going on, in the sense of the continuing need for a physical as opposed to a psychological reaction to the events.

The role of the tape-recorder

For a number of months after the return to therapy, this split between a rather light-hearted/jovial and sombre/persecuted mode of relating was in evidence in most sessions. The tape-recorder played a key role in this. Jim would often begin the sessions in a jovial mood where the whole affect was quite light-hearted, but quite often, for reasons that I could not always ascertain, the tone of the sessions would change. He seemed to become frightened, and either before or after this change in mood he would ask again and again what the recorder was for. I have not used a recorder before, and obviously in these sessions it had a special significance. At the beginning of his return to therapy, I was interested to see how things would develop. What seemed to emerge was that, far from the recorder being thought of as neutral or unobtrusive, its presence had to be engaged with actively. My response to his questions was factual and interpretive, focusing on the use of the tape-recorder to validate what really happened and how difficult it might sometimes be to differentiate between what happened and what he thought might have happened. After several months, he said to me "You didn't really do anything to me did you?", and this led to a fruitful and serious discussion of the course of events and just how confused he sometimes became as regards his memory of events. His supposition when in the accusatory frame of mind that I had sent him to sleep through the use of a drug obviously added to the confusion and the difficulty of differentiating fantasy from reality. It is also important to note that drugs were thought to be part of the original abusive experience.

Discussion

I felt that Jim's confusion was genuine and, to use a very apposite expression, that he had been an "honest liar". In a way that has obvious parallels to the description of his own mother's state of mind, I think that, when he made the allegation, Jim himself genuinely believed in what he was saying. It is, I believe, this quality that crucially differentiates this patient from the first three described above and it is this same quality that led to the allegation being acted upon.

In furthering my understanding of this, I found Michael Sinason's (1993) concept of internal co-habitation or co-residency of two minds in one body very useful as a working model. He starts from Freud's concept of the way in which, if an ego is overwhelmed by demands of the external world, a process of detachment can take place whereby part of the ego then remains orientated by the demands of the external reality while the detached part lives in the world of illusions (Freud, 1924e). Rosenfeld's (1971) elaboration of this "illustrated how an internal psychic organization can be built up within the ego which usurps the functions of the ego and turns them to destructive ends. Intelligence is thereby turned to the service of destructiveness; and achievement is conceived of solely in terms of the domination and subjugation of others to the narcissistic aims of the ill ego" (M. Sinason, 1993, p. 209; cf. Patient B above). Rosenfeld develops the notion of the internal gang, whereby treatment is then conceived of as disentangling the residual sane parts of the ego from the destructive narcissistic parts. Sinason expands this concept, describing how he conceives of treatment as fostering the development in the patient of a genuine capability for making decisions in life which adequately take account of the needs of his own mind as well as that of the co-habitee. He describes how treatment

> cannot be achieved by premature injunctions for the patient to "be responsible" and will not occur if the patient has an attitude of wishing to be rid of the co-habitee or of condemnation and resentment. One important part of the development of genuine interest and concern for the co-habitee comes though attention to the ways in which the mind of the co-habitee is

often using concrete symbolic equations instead of symbolism and is therefore unable to think symbolically, which constitutes a significant degree of thought disorder and disability. This in turn leads to a recognition that destructive consequences do not always rise from destructive aims. A mind that is incapable of symbolic functioning can be urgent, ruthless and expedient and thereby injure others directly as a result of these disabilities. [p. 219]

The links with the differentiation between "acting out" and "remembering" will be apparent, as will the difficulties of the professional network in moving from the psychical to the physical domain, for at that point the network can be said to have been in the service of this disabled part of the mind.

Further clinical material illustrates this more clearly. Jim would often play at the sink. He would almost always ask me to come close when engaged in this activity, and, though I would explore this with him, it was not possible fully to ascertain the reasons for this. The split between light-hearted/jovial and sombre/persecuting was again apparent in his play. He would often seem happily engaged but then suddenly become frightened. Exploration by me led to little clarification of this. In one session, he leapt back in real terror, eventually being able to say that he was frightened of "the monster in the sink . . . look, there are its eyes". He was pointing to the plug, and, as the last drops of water went down the pipe, I could imagine how they could be seen as eyes. The "trigger" for his anxiety and his reaction was unusually in the open, and we could discuss his confusion. He then put a flannel over the plug. It helped momentarily, but he then said, "but it's still in there, only covered up".

This provides an illustration of Jim's mental processes and, at this point in time, the lack of symbolic functioning. There are obvious parallels between this and the allegation of abuse and, perhaps most poignantly with reference to the tape-recorder, his fear that the abuser was still lurking within me. There are also important differences, the most pertinent of which is that with this material I was able to take it up psychically and think it through with him.

Looking for triggers

What, though, of the specific aetiology of the allegation of abuse? Why did this particular child respond in this way? I think further clues to understanding this can be found in the experience of holiday breaks and the primitive, infantile feelings that may be aroused at those times. In order to understand the material, it was important to think about the ways in which Jim's earliest and most primitive interactions with his primary objects would have left their traces, exerting a powerful but disabling and destructive influence upon the form and structure of his personality.

The first holiday break after his return was dominated by a planned change of foster-parents. Following the next break (Easter and the anniversary of the time at which he had alleged the abuse), Jim did not return for his first session and I was left waiting for him—very anxiously! I later telephoned the foster-home and was informed that the session had been forgotten! At the next session, when Jim did return he was physically sick on the way. This had not happened at any other time, and I believe that this and the previously forgotten session were more than coincidence and had to do with the anniversary of the allegation. In the following session with Jim, I made an interpretation along these lines, and he nodded in agreement.

Some months later, at the last session before the summer break, the recorder again became the focus of his attention. Jim had become quite aggressive, and I had been interpreting this material with regards to the impending summer break when he responded by saying that I could turn the recorder off. This, I think, provides a vital clue, as it demonstrates how in his mind he links the experience of my "turning the sessions off" with that of being able to turn the recorder off and, presumably, in his phantasy, then taking away the recorder's protective capacity and leaving him open to further abuse.

Freud presumed childhood love to be boundless: "It demands exclusive possession, it is not content with less than all. But it has a second characteristic: it has in point of fact no aim and is incapable of obtaining complete satisfaction; and principally for this reason it is doomed to end in disappointment and to give place to a hostile attitude".

The material that Jim presented in the sessions does then lend itself to linking the allegation of abuse to these hostile, early infantile feelings, reactivated in therapy at the holiday breaks but jaundiced by his real-life experiences of gross sexual abuse and a problematic infancy with a mother with severe mental health problems. He has a long, repetitive history of changing primary carers; the break from his mother was because of concerns as regards her capacity to look after her children and allegations of sexual abuse. His history links separations to allegations of sexual abuse and this seemed to be the destructive quality that was acted upon at the point at which the allegation was made.

Conclusion

In this chapter I have focused on a specific situation—a false allegation of sexual abuse—in which a patient's communications and memories of a particular event seemed to transform that event radically—and with potentially drastic results. Through an exploration of work with a number of other patients, who for varying reasons have made varying allegations of abuse against myself as their therapist, I have tried to consider and differentiate between different frames of mind and, especially, to explore some of the reasons behind this particular allegation being believed and acted upon in contrast to others that were not. The very fact that the allegation was believed did seem to throw some light upon the patient's own pathology and his own belief, at that point, that something had really happened. This belief had a very real impact upon the professional network, resulting in a full diagnostic enquiry and, because professional abuse does take place, this could be considered as necessary "acting out". But such "acting out" can reinforce the disturbed part of the patient's personality and is a most disturbing experience for the therapist, the patient, and other members of the professional network.

CHAPTER NINE

Syndromitis, false or repressed memories?

Steven Rose

In this chapter, Steven Rose provides us with a deceptively simple account of how memory works. He presents a thoughtfully sceptical description of "syndromitis"—the increase of quasi-medical categories—as well as a review of the works of Drs Loftus and Ofshe.

Anew and dangerous disease is sweeping America. I call it *syndromitis*—the arbitrary invention of quasi-medical categories to suit almost any deviation from what is perceived as the norm: the ideal state of middle-performing, middlingly happy, and 30-something-aged Americans. So we have attention-deficit disorder (ADD), dissociative identity disorder (DID), age-associated memory deficit, Munchausen's syndrome-by-proxy, post-traumatic stress disorder—and dozens more, clamouring for status in the clinician's bible: the *Diagnostic and Statistical Manual of Mental Disorders*, now into its fourth version.

A shorter version of this chapter originally appeared in *The New York Times*.

Fashionable names for these categories change with alarming speed. ADD used to be hyperkinesia, then hyperactivity; DID was not so long ago multiple personality disorder. Once such categories have been invented, the tendency for clinicians and therapists to search them out in their clients bandwagons, for there are papers to be written and careers to be made in defining, as much as there are in treating, the conditions. Fashion is helped along by middle America's rewriting of the Constitution: it is no longer merely the pursuit but the possession of happiness which has become an inalienable right. Happiness itself is no longer to be defined in terms of the Four Freedoms specified by the founders of the United Nations (if it were, many U.S. citizens would be profoundly unhappy)—but by a relatively new right, that to sexual content.

Those who are unhappy have a limited range of choices. They can blame their circumstances, such as poverty, racism, patriarchy; they can blame their genes; or they can blame their parents. The first is the hardest, because it demands social action, and it isn't easy to decide who to sue—though judging by the way in which children have been suing their parents for pre-natal negligence in recent cases, this gap in America's pursuit of legalized rights will soon be filled. Either of the other choices offers therapeutic prospects: with them one enters the world of Prozac or of the talking therapies, both richly possessed of syndromes available for the taking.

Enter the two most recent—the mirror-images of repressed memory syndrome and false memory syndrome—both of which, if I understand their history aright, emerged in the United States during the 1980s and, as is the way of such fashions, have over the last few years appeared on this side of the Atlantic. Riding on the back of the shocking discovery of widespread child abuse and father–child incest, a number of therapists have claimed that clients consulting them for quite other reasons, ranging from eating disorders to unhappy marriages, owe their present distress to early but now forgotten abuse. As many outsiders to therapy such as myself have often wryly suggested, patients in talk-therapy tend to adapt their problems to the theories of the therapists (the history runs back to Freud and earlier), and in due course the "repressed" memories are "recovered", often to the horror of the patient, and usually to the enormous distress of the parents, who will strenuously deny the claims. The patient may find comfort in the support of other survivors; the alleged abusers have, in their turn, formed associations to counter what they see as false memories. The resulting court cases, with expert witnesses testifying on both sides, have attracted international publicity and huge legal costs.

Two recent books, the principal authors of which, Drs Loftus and Ofshe, are respectively a psychologist specializing in human memory and a social psychologist, have now taken on the task of demystifying the claims of repressed memory. Both authors have been actively engaged in defending those charged with abuse (and worse) on the basis of recovered memories, and their two books cover much the same ground. The same cases—indeed the identical transcripts—appear in both books, and each author generously acknowledges the other. Before leaving the calm of the psychology laboratory for the morass of real human experience, Dr Loftus's research (Loftus & Ketcham, 1994) had been focused on the accuracy of memory and, indeed, in a number of now famous experiments had shown how easy it is to "implant" memories or distort a person's recollection of even the recent past. In the best-known version of the experiments, she arranged for adults to describe to children in their care a fictitious account of having been lost in a shopping mall, and she recorded how, later, the children claimed that such an event had really occurred, giving graphic and detailed descriptions of what had occurred. Dr Ofshe, by contrast, has focused on issues of psychic coercion, of brainwashing, especially in the context of cults (Ofshe & Watters, 1994). The descriptions both of them give of the "therapeutic" practices by which memories are recovered are a frightening indictment of at least some members of the burgeoning therapy industry in the United States, its "heads-I-win, tails-you-lose" approach of moral and political rectitude and its capacities for self-delusion, though neither author falls into the trap of denying that child sexual abuse can and does occur and can be, to all intents and purposes, forgotten by the victim. Of the two, Dr Ofshe's book is the more academic and wide-ranging, taking in memories of satanic cults and even Holocaust denial, whilst Dr Loftus's account is more a personal testimony of her own, initially reluctant, engagement with the issues and the defendants.

In both cases, their rebuttal of the claims made by some of those who have recovered such "repressed memories" from their patients is based on a mix of evidence. There are disturbing accounts of the bullying tactics used by these therapists in their attempts to "recover" the memory, including assertions that the stronger the initial denial the more probable it is that there is something there to be denied (i.e. that where there is no smoke, there must be a fire) and their attempts forcibly to shoehorn the variety of human experience into tightly fitting theory. There is the inherent improbability of some of the repressed memories "recovered", including their expansion during therapy from initially relatively minor episodes to full-blown charges of murder and cannibalism involving entire conspiracies of family members. There is also the evidence derived from laboratory studies and real-life experiences of how verifiable memories can be confabulated but are rarely lost and then recovered from zero, as is the case in some of the reported cases.

That these issues are alive and serious in the United Kingdom as well is indicated by two recent events. The first is yet another widely publicized "satanic abuse" case, which seems to have begun with a charge being brought against a 14-year-old boy with a record of sexual offences, but then burgeoned over the course of a year of investigation into claims by a number of children to have been subjected to bizarre ritual abuses by several neighbouring families. The case ended, as eventually have most such others, in acquittals for all the families concerned. The children's allegations simply could not be sustained. The second is the report on "false memory syndrome" by the British Psychological Society (Morton et al., 1995) following a study apparently requested by the 550-strong False Memory Society. The report, which is likely to satisfy neither the members of the society nor those who make the strongest claims for the reality of repressed and recovered memory, takes a middle position: memories can be "lost" and later "recovered" under particular circumstances, but they are clearly also liable to considerable plasticity.

The problem is that there are two different types of truth: historic truth—or what actually happened—and narrative truth—a person's account of his or her remembered experience. If human memories were like computer memories, neatly filed somewhere on a disc and waiting only to be called up, the two might be identical. Indeed, this is what some of the theorists of recovered memory seem to believe. But our memories are not like this; they are biological, labile, dynamic. Those of us who, like me, study the brain processes involved in learning believe that memories are initially laid down in the brain in the form of changes in the patterns of connections between nerve cells, the 10^{15} synaptic connections of the human brain. These changes occur via a complex biochemical pathway, but the meaning of any pattern is embedded not within the individual cells, but within the brain as a system. A simple computer model of memory would assume that once the pattern had been laid down, it remained there for the duration of a memory, waiting only to be reactivated—and indeed this is how some proponents of artificial intelligence still try to model memory. But the biological evidence is different. Patterns of connections are labile and change over time; memories are not localized in particular brain regions but distributed and represented in the brain by fluctuating patterns of coherent neural activity. This means that remembering is not a passive process of simply reactivating circuits, but requires real work—it is, literally, re-membering. At least one psychologist of memory, Ewald Tulving (1991), has gone so far as to argue that memories do not exist as "stores" in the brain at all, but are actually created by the work of re-membering (Tulving has a word for it—*ecphorising*). Whilst few of us would go that far in denying the stability of brain representations of external events, what is minimally clear is the dynamic nature of both learning and re-membering.

What all this might mean in the context of therapy is that once a therapist has recovered—or induced—a "memory", it is *that* memory which now becomes inscribed in the brain's synapses, and what is recalled next time is no longer the original event (if that ever occurred) but the *memory* of that event. That is, the new memory has become biologically real for its possessor, independently of how it got there. In the absence of some independent verification procedure, there is no way of deciding between a survivor's claim that his or her new narrative memory is real, and the father's that it is false. The legal world deals in neat dichotomies of truth and falsehood, madness and badness. But we humans do not

find it easy to live by such distinctions, either biologically or socially. The past may be the key to the present, as many therapists
believe, but happiness—if that is the goal—and even survival itself
may require that we let the dead bury the dead. None of this
means that we should be allowed to ignore the enormity of the
horrors that some parents—fathers, predominantly—wreak upon
their children. But it does mean that we cannot and must not take
the claims for memory emerging through therapy at simple face
value. All of this places particular responsibilities upon therapists.
It reinforces both my own relief that I am able to study memory in
the relative tranquillity of the laboratory, and predominantly in
non-human animals, rather than in the pain of the consulting-
room, and my belief that some of these problems would diminish
were there a proper certification procedure required of all who
claim therapeutic competence.

CHAPTER TEN

Terror in the consulting-room— memory, trauma, and dissociation

Phil Mollon

In this chapter, Phil Mollon explores both psychoanalytic and psychological theories of repression and memory as well as taking us into painful clinical illustrations.

"The idea that our minds can play tricks on us, leading us to believe in a distorted reality, even in fantasy and confabulation, is deeply disturbing. If we can't trust our own minds to tell us the truth, what is left to trust?"

Loftus & Ketcham, 1994, p. 68

When I completed training in analytic psychotherapy over a decade ago, I thought that the task of my work was to analyse the structures and conflicts within the patient's mind as they unfolded within the transference. In the last few years, as I have tried to help people more damaged than those

---

A longer version of this chapter appears in Mollon (1996a).

usually attending a psychotherapy service, the cosy security of that tried and tested way of working has been shattered; my sense of reality and sanity has been repeatedly assaulted by communications of bizarre and horrifying memories, or apparent memories, for which my training had not prepared me. With these more injured and traumatized individuals, it is as if flashback *memory*, or *memory-like* material, violently intrudes, smashing the usual framework, assumptions, and epistemological basis of analytic practice.

Let me briefly state my present position, having digested these experiences and reflected at length upon the clinical and research memory literature (see also Mollon, 1995, 1996a, 1996b, 1998). I believe the following to be the case. False or pseudo-memories of childhood are possible; true memories of childhood trauma are also possible. A person may be able to avoid thinking about these memories for certain periods (a phenomenon that cognitive therapists call "cognitive avoidance"), and this may be combined with mechanisms of pretence and denial to make the memories unavailable. Later, in response to certain cues, or when in a safe environment, the memories may intrude into awareness; sometimes people seek therapy *because* memories have begun to intrude. Memory is prone to error; we are continually interpreting and remixing our perceptions of past events. Between the extremes of "true" and "false" memory lies a vast area of uncertainty and ambiguity. One task of the analytic therapist is to tolerate this uncertainty and help the patient tolerate this too. Because it is impossible, as listening and responding participants in the analytic process, not to influence the emerging narrative, it is important to be open to a variety of possible understandings of the patient's history and development. Procedures intended to elicit memories of trauma may be inadvisable because (1) pseudo-memories may be encouraged and (2) the patient may be retraumatized in the process. Understanding the problems of memory in clinical practice requires the cooperation of psychoanalysis and cognitive psychology.

Psychoanalytic views of trauma and memory

About 100 years ago, Freud was struggling with the relative importance of reality-trauma and fantasy—and in particular the truth status of recovered memory. For example, in a letter to Abraham in 1907, he wrote:

> A proportion of the sexual traumas reported by patients are or may be phantasies ... disentangling them from the so frequent genuine ones is not easy. [Abraham & Freud, 1965]

As we know, Freud's attention moved from the impact of actual sexual abuse, and memories of this, to the role of the instincts and fantasy and, in particular, to the Oedipus complex. Blass and Simon (1994) describe the stages in Freud's development and discarding of his original seduction-trauma theories and his painful struggle with issues of evidence and truth. Simon (1992), in commenting on the decline of psychoanalytic interest in actual trauma and sexual abuse, in a paper entitled "Incest—see under Oedipus Complex: The History of an Error in Psychoanalysis", writes:

> I believe much of what Freud had begun to observe and theorise about incest, and much of what he might have elaborated, migrated to the area of the primal scene, the psychoanalytic trauma par excellence. ... Primal Scene thus served as a distraction from, or defence against, the further awareness of the trauma of actual sexual abuse of children by parents. [p. 971]

Meanwhile, Ferenczi continued to emphasize both trauma in the genesis of mental disorder and the modifications of analytic technique which he felt were necessary to reach these deeper levels of warded-off experience. This conflicted with Freud's position. In a letter to Freud in 1929, Ferenczi summarized his views:

> In all cases where I penetrated deeply enough, I found uncovered the traumatic-hysterical basis of the illness.
>
> Where the patient and I succeeded in this, the therapeutic effect was far more significant. In many cases I had to recall previously "cured" patients for further treatment. [Ferenczi, 1933]

He also complained of a trend in psychoanalysis towards "overestimating the role of fantasy, and underestimating that of traumatic reality, in pathogenesis".

On the whole, analysts who have emphasized actual trauma have been criticized, often fiercely, as Ferenczi was by Freud. Greenacre (1971), in commenting on the response to her earlier writings on pre-oedipal trauma, which were not specifically concerned with incest, wrote:

> The amount of resistance to my findings took me by surprise, especially the attitude expressed several times by colleagues that my work attempted to undermine the importance of the Oedipus complex.

Winnicott's views on the facilitating environment and on environmental failure, written in reaction to the emphasis of Melanie Klein on innate phantasy, stirred controversy and considerable hostility, but they were perhaps more accepted because he was emphasizing inadvertent trauma rather than gross and deliberate abuse.

Contemporary analysts still vary considerably over what credence is to be given to suggestions of actual sexual abuse and trauma. For example, a group of analysts who heard material from the following psychoanalytic therapy were quite divided over whether the patient might have been sexually abused or not.

The patient shows the following characteristics. She frequently experiences terrors that the male therapist will sexually assault her. For this reason, she will not lie on the couch. Instead, she sits in a chair, which she requested be moved near the door for ease of escape. She often insists on leaving the door open so that she can run away easily if the therapist were to attack her. She is very afraid of men generally. She avoids wearing any clothes that might be seen as sexually provocative. Sometimes she enters a dissociative state and reports in a childlike manner experiences of sexual abuse and violent assault. On occasion, she resorts to action and screaming rather than words and will appear to be enacting scenes of sexual assault. She describes what she calls flashbacks of sexual assault—evoked, for example, by the sensation of a toothbrush in her mouth—and she becomes very frightened and flips into a state of dissociation and disorientation. She presented a series of dreams in which men are breaking into the house she is in; in one of these a pole is thrown through the window; in some dreams she develops amazing strength to repel these men—and in one dream she thrusts an umbrella violently down someone's throat. She believes that she was sexually abused as a child, but she has no clear and visual memories of this.

Was she sexually abused or is the imagery of sexual attack a sexualized form of the patient's own violent wish to intrude and to control the therapist, now experienced in projection as coming back at her? It is the question of who thrust the umbrella phallus down whose throat first. Other possibilities were also suggested, but the idea that she may have been literally sexually abused tended to be the least favoured option.

This ambivalence amongst analysts about the reality or otherwise of sexual abuse is mirrored by that amongst patients. Van Leeuwen, in a paper entitled "Resistances in the Treatment of a Sexually Molested 6-Year-Old Girl" (1988), describes how the impulse to tell may occur in sudden bursts, unexpectedly, and may be followed by retraction and denial. Non-verbal re-enactments were more frequent than verbal disclosure.

Mechanisms of memory and amnesia: what do we really know?

In all the tangle of arguments around the issues of recovered and false memory, there is much intelligent reasoning and a number of relevant studies but precious little firm knowledge when it comes to the mechanisms of memory we encounter in clinical work.

Repression has never been experimentally demonstrated in the laboratory. However, there is nothing novel or implausible about the notion of avoidance, repression, or dissociation of memories of trauma and their recovery, whether in the context of psychological therapy or in response to some other life circumstances. Clinical and naturalistic research (as opposed to that based in a laboratory) that has looked at survivors of abuse has indeed found evidence suggestive of avoidance of memory for trauma (e.g. Briere & Conte, 1993; Feldman-Summers & Pope, 1994; Herman & Schatzow, 1987;

Loftus et al., 1994; Williams, 1994a). Pope and Hudson (1995) have criticized these studies, arguing that independent documented evidence corroborating the "memory" is required to support the concept of repression. Such evidence is reported by Schooler (1994) and Williams (1995). Few in the field deny that motivated avoidance of memory is possible. The debate is about the reliability of recovered memory.

In 1994, two books were published by two memory experts: *Unchained Memories* by Lenore Terr, who is a psychiatrist who has made longitudinal studies of the memory of trauma victims, and *The Myth of Repressed Memory* by Elizabeth Loftus and Katherine Ketcham—Loftus is an academic psychologist specializing in memory research. The books are strikingly similar in style, both highly readable—and both describe the same murder case where the crucial and sole piece of evidence was an adult's flashback memory of her father bludgeoning a child to death. Terr, arguing for the prosecution, argued that there was every reason to believe that the memory was true and claimed that traumatic memories are retained in particularly vivid detail. Loftus, witness for the defence, disagreed, arguing that there was every reason to doubt the reliability of the apparent memory, and she claimed that her research showed that trauma particularly interfered with the accuracy of memory. The jury believed Terr. Two memory experts, two divergent views.

Commenting on experiments by Loftus and others which indicate ways in which memory can be falsified in the laboratory, Terr (1994) writes, rather dismissively:

> Despite the interesting points in the Loftus research, psychological experiments on university students do not duplicate in any way the clinician's observation. What comes from the memory lab does not apply well to the perception, storage, and retrieval of such things as childhood murders, rapes or kidnappings. Trauma sets up new rules for memory. . . . You can't simulate murders without terrorising your research subjects. Experiments on college students do not simulate clinical instances of trauma. And they have little to do with childhood itself. [p. 52]

Loftus disagrees, arguing that experimental psychologists study the basic processes of memory formation, storage, and retrieval, which *can* be generalized to real life. She emphasizes the essential permeability of memory, described as "flexible and superimposable, a panoramic blackboard with an endless supply of chalk and erasers" (1994, p. 3). Actually, I find Loftus to be the more cautious of the two writers, sensitive to the dilemmas of the clinician but emphasizing uncertainty in evaluating memory.

Whilst Terr certainly believes that false memories are possible, she argues that if recovered memory is associated with signs and symptoms of trauma, then this is evidence that the memory may contain truth:

> If a child is exposed to a shocking, frightening, painful or overexciting event, he or she will exhibit psychological signs of having had the experience. The child will reenact aspects of the terrible episode and may complain of physical sensations similar to those originally felt. The child will fear a repetition of the episode, and will often feel generally and unduly pessimistic about the future. . . . If on the other hand, a child is exposed only to a frightening rumour, . . . to the symptoms of another victim of trauma, the child may pick up a symptom or two . . . but will not suffer a cluster of symptoms and signs. [1994, p. 161]

Perhaps so—but the fact that an apparent memory is consistent with a cluster of symptoms and signs does not prove that the particular memory is true. The "memory" could be a fantasy, congruent with a deep schema of the mind but not containing literal truth. Such a memory could be structurally true but literally false.

How is the experience of trauma processed and stored in memory? The theorizing of some cognitive psychologists, such as Schactel, Bruner, Postman, Neisser, Piaget, suggests that memory is encoded in different cognitive modes during the earliest months—in enactive and iconic modes, as opposed to linguistic (Greenberg & van der Kolk, 1987). This reveals the possibility of a blocking of the processing of trauma into the symbolic language necessary for cognitive retrieval—so that a person could then experience "unspeakable terror" or "nameless dread" (van der Kolk, 1996). We might also then expect the possibility of the partial reliving of affective and somatosensory components of traumatic memories, without the symbolic and linguistic representations necessary to place the trauma in its historic context. Such partial flashbacks could be reactivated by affective, auditory, or visual cues—for example, the way a person may be precipitated into a state of rage and terror whilst having intercourse with his or her partner. The caution must be added, however, that as soon as the attempt is made to create a verbal narrative out of these somatosensory fragments, distortion and confabulation may begin.

A study by Terr (1991) has a bearing on these issues. She found that amongst twenty children with documented histories of early trauma, none could give a verbal description of events before the age of 2½ years, but eighteen of these showed evidence of a traumatic memory in their behaviour and play; for example, a child who in the first two years of life had been sexually molested by a babysitter could not at age 5 remember or name the babysitter and also denied any knowledge of being abused, but in his play he enacted scenes that exactly replicated a pornographic movie made by the babysitter. In another example, a 5-year-old child who had been sexually and pornographically abused in a day centre between age 15 and 18 months was amnesic of these events but reported a "funny feeling" in her "tummy" whenever a finger was pointed at her; photographs confiscated from the centre showed an erect penis pointing at her stomach.

Terr has studied traumatized children over many years. She finds that recall for "single-blow" traumas in an otherwise trauma-free environment, which she calls Type I traumas, are usually recalled with startling precision and detail. By contrast, Type II traumas, which involve repeated brutalization, are processed very differently. She writes (1991):

> The defenses and coping operations used in the Type II disorders of childhood—massive denial, repression, dissociation, self-anaesthesia, self-hypnosis, identification with aggressor, and aggression turned against the self—often lead to profound character changes. . . . Children who experience Type II traumas often forget. They may forget whole segments of childhood. . . . Repeatedly brutalized, benumbed children employ massive denial. [p. 16]

What Terr seems to mean here is that repeatedly abused children develop generally disturbed minds, within which memory is disrupted.

My own impression is that the fundamental mental defence against overwhelming trauma is dissociation: this is the child flipping into a state of auto-hypnosis, thinking "I am not here—this is not happening to me", etc. A patient who came to see me specifically claiming a history of ritual abuse could hardly get any words out in our first meeting. Eventually she gasped, falteringly, "It's difficult to speak because I'm not here." When she did in later sessions talk of early experiences of extreme horror, she would refer to her child self as "she". On one occasion, after giving me a very fragmented and incoherent account of an experience of a mock operation in which she had been told that "eyes and ears" with special powers had been placed inside her so that the abusers would always know what she was thinking, saying, or doing, she repeatedly muttered the words "eyes no body". It took some minutes for me to grasp that she was telling me that she had gone into a state of dissociation in which she experienced herself as just two eyes without a body. She was gradually able to explain that she had learnt from an early age to get out of her body when she was subjected to extreme pain; in her imagination, she would, for example, escape into a crack in the ceiling, or into a lightbulb— apparently using some kind of spontaneous auto-hypnosis. Often she would tell me of some early experience of abuse and trauma and subsequently have no apparent memory of having told me, although she would acknowledge a memory of the events described.

This material gives just a hint of the ways in which the consciousness and memory of a abused victim may be scrambled with the deliberate intention of creating maximal difficulty in remembering, in telling, and in being believed. If we add to this the possibilities of abuse before language is acquired, confusions induced by the use of drugs administered by abusers (as is sometimes alleged), and the natural intermingling of reality, dreams, and fantasy in the child part of the mind, as well as the unconscious use of images as metaphors, then we can see what a devil of a job we have in sorting out what really went on!

A patient with a dissociative disorder pointed out to me that it is relatively easy to persuade a survivor of childhood trauma that her or his memories are false, because these may be encoded in a dissociated state—so that the main personality does not recognize them as her or his own. If you try to imagine the experience of a fragmented dissociative personality, it is like having other people living inside your body who claim to have certain memories, but you have no way of knowing whether these are true. Moreover, the narrative of abuse may be presented by the patient in a frightened, confused, and child-like state of mind—dissociated from the adult state of mind—so that no rational and adult discussion with the "narrator" is possible.

A clinical and theoretical tangle indeed! There are many voices in the memory debate, but none who can reliably lead the clinician out of the maze. The more one hears, the more one is confused, as each claim is challenged by a counterclaim. A major report by the American Psychological Association (1996) offers no consensus but degenerates into bad-tempered argument between opposing "camps".

Trauma, abuse, and the sense of reality

A phenomenon that I have observed with a number of patients is that where a person appears to have been repeatedly traumatized in childhood, he or she is often left with an unreliable sense of reality. If asked, the person may acknowledge that he or she sometimes has difficulty distinguishing whether something really happened or whether it was a dream. Over time, their account of "memories" of childhood events may vary—perhaps with a recurring theme but with details and persons involved changing; details of one scene of abuse seem be transposed and remixed to form new scenes, making identification of the true original scene extremely difficult. It is as if repeated childhood trauma may lead not just to repression or other forms of motivated amnesia, as is sometimes suggested, but also to an even more *unreliable* memory and sense of reality.

Why might this be? One possibility is that if auto-hypnotic dissociation is a primary defensive response to repeated trauma, a person might then become prone to enter hypnoid states of mind in which judgement of reality is impaired. In such a state a person could be auto-hypnotically generating false memory narratives that mix elements of truth and confabulation, just as may happen in "memory" recall in induced hypnosis.

A further possibility is suggested by a bit of Lacanian theory. With regard to the relationship of the mind to the outer world, Lacan (1977) postulates three orders or dimensions: the Real, the Imaginary, and the Symbolic. The Real is essentially unknowable; for example, a biological need can only be known through an image or a word, but not directly. The Imaginary is the realm of images, fantasies, and wish-fulfillments—the world of the dream, which follows the primary process forms of thought. The Symbolic order is arrived at through entry into the shared social world of language and culture; no one can avoid this transition from the Imaginary to the Symbolic without being psychotic. Lacan saw this achievement being structured through the oedipal crisis, through acceptance of the incest taboo and the "Law of the Father", which forbids both mother and child to repossess each other and which therefore represents a fundamental separation between fantasy and reality. The child's identity and sense of boundaries and reality requires that he or she be excluded from the "primal scene" of the parental intercourse.

In the light of these Lacanian insights, what happens if there is incest with the father or if the child is included in the primal scene? It would follow that then there can be no proper entry into the Symbolic, since the "law-giver" is the "law-breaker". There will be no clear sense of where the "Law" is situated. Whilst perhaps escaping full psychosis, the person's sense of reality will be defective. He or she will be immersed in the Imaginary, as if trapped in a dream. The boundary between "inside" and "outside" will be unclear. Internal dream and external reality will confusingly intermingle.

Similar problems may arise if there is cult ritual abuse. If we accept the hypothesis that there are indeed perverse cults, then some children may be secretly exposed to bizarre activities that could normally only occur in a dream or nightmare and are totally outside the shared language and culture of society. Such experiences could not be spoken about and therefore could not be given words and would be foreclosed from consciousness. If primitive fantasy and reality meet up in this way, then the outer world becomes identified with an archetype in which the Terrible Mother and the Terrible Father are perceived as real. Again, the barrier between fantasy and reality is blown away.

Clinical illustration

Some years ago, when I knew nothing about ritual abuse, a patient told me of a strange and horrifying event. No "memory recovery" techniques were used. As far as I am aware the patient had not spoken with any other survivors of this kind of abuse, nor read about it. The account that emerged was a surprise and a profound shock, which left me bewildered and confused.

> Helen was a 40-year-old schoolteacher of French origin; she was in once-weekly psychoanalytic therapy because of severe and chronic disturbance of affect and interpersonal relationships. From the beginning, she had presented extensive material relating to sexual abuse by her father. There was no "recovered memory" here—she appeared never to have been amnesic for the abuse and even described it continuing into her adult life. There were also minor hints of more peculiar elements—for example, her father's apparent claim to have paranormal powers, her belief that he used to drug her, and memories of a period in her childhood when disgusting objects, including animal limbs, were put through the letter box (possibly at a time when her parents, now both dead, were attempting to leave the cult they had been involved with). For a long time these allusions to more bizarre experiences remained obscure.

> There were often indications in the transference of early experiences of sadism. She often perceived me as wanting to control her and repeatedly humiliate her. If I seemed to understand her, she felt that this was only in order to gain more opportunity to hurt her and to control her mind. Sometimes she feared that I would somehow be in league with her father. Her experience of the world seemed to be pervaded by cruelty, terror, and her own intense rage.

> One session she reported a frightening experience. During the week, she had been opening a jar of spaghetti sauce in her

kitchen and had accidentally dropped it; some of the sauce had splashed up the walls. On seeing this, Helen had run out of the kitchen in a state of great terror, feeling that it reminded her of something but not knowing what. Subsequently she had recalled a vivid childhood "memory" of a terrifying scene in the woods—the details of which need not concern us here, except to say that it was of quite a different order to anything that she had described before.

Unravelling of image, affect, and narrative

What was I to make of this apparent memory? Had she recovered a memory or constructed a delusion? Whatever the origin of its content, whether in experience or fantasy, this sudden emergence of detailed imagery and narrative seems typical of "flashbacks" of ritual abuse, which are often preceded by much material regarding sexual abuse; the ritual abuse material emerges later, as if unravelling from a different layer of mental storage. The imagery is often highly detailed and shocking, and its occurrence is in itself traumatic and evokes denial; for example, in the session following this, Helen was preoccupied with a wish not to believe her own account. She experienced urges to punish herself, to slash her wrists, and asked me in a childlike voice whether I now wanted her to kill herself. The power of the processes of scrambling or blocking of memory (if that is what it was) in these cases is illustrated by Helen's account of how she and her sister used to have discussions about whether they should go to the police, but they could never remember what it was they were meant to be going to the police about; they knew something had happened but could never remember what. She told me that she felt she had always remembered what had happened but had not before been able to connect the memories with words. Helen described how certain associative cues had in the past triggered terror—for example, her first church communion, and drinking a bowl of lukewarm soup—but she had not been able to make the connection consciously.

There were other features of dissociation in her presentation; for example, she described a split between the one who came to the session and the one who remembered all the horrors when she was alone. Similarly, I noticed that on occasion she would talk in a way that gave no hint whatsoever of ritual abuse and perversion, and at other times her discourse would be filled with allusions to this.

THE DYNAMICS OF COMMUNICATING THIS MATERIAL

Did I go in search of this material? Did I expect to find it? No. My response to hearing this and similar material has contained elements of shock, disbelief, dread, and terror—and confusion—a sense of difficulty in assessing reality. These, I suspect, are typical countertransference reactions to a communicated experience that is like an assault on one's sense of reality.

I experienced the countertransference as one of a split ego state, part of my mind believing the accounts and another part thinking they are preposterous. In this kind of material, there often seems to be an intermingling of elements that are shocking and believable, with those that are unbelievable. Some survivors of abuse networks claim that this is a deliberate ploy to undermine credibility of witnesses. Inherent in perversion appears to be a delight in confusion and subterfuge, playing tricks with reality and the sense of reality, the interweaving of truth and lies. A quality of "now you see it, now you don't" seems to pervade both the clinical experiences and the criminal investigations.

I am certain that Helen could not have told me about these things until she felt that I could be receptive to them. Moreover, until she told me, she could not tell herself. Her perception of the look of horror on my face when she told me of the events greatly troubled her, and she frequently referred to this in the years following. She complained that I looked so shaken that I was of no help to her in coping with her own reactions. She felt that she must protect me from further trauma, fearing that I would not tolerate more revelations, whilst at the same time needing to know that I could be emotionally affected by her experiences. It was important to show her, through interpretation, that I could bear to hear what she needed to tell me and could think about it with her.

Helen made much progress, but in the later stages of the therapy she was aware of a continuing struggle against forgetting, recognizing her own wish to forget. She remained preoccupied with her fear that I might forget—her point being that *somebody* had to remember. She pointed out with great dismay that I did seem to forget some details of the terrible experiences that she described—and when I checked my notes I realized that she was correct.

Was it true? Did Helen really witness such serious crimes? Are there perverse cults? How could the account ever be corroborated? What is the best way of responding to such an account? How would the therapy have developed if I had disbelieved that there could be literal truth in what she remembered—could she have still got better? I do not know the answer to any of these questions, but I did not disbelieve her—whilst accepting that I could never know objectively the historical truth and that I might be mistaken. On what basis did I believe her account could contain some literal truth, bearing in mind that I have no evidence outside of the consulting-room? On what basis do we believe or disbelieve anyone? Could the whole narrative be a gigantic confabulation? If so, what on earth was its source—and what would be the motive behind the production of a narrative that filled the patient with shame and guilt and the therapist with despair?

Epistemological terror

I suggest three forms of terror in the consulting-room.

We may experience terror as we empathize with the patient in the reliving of early trauma and terror.

We can also experience terror if a part of the patient is identified with the abusers and attempts to terrorize us, a form of projective identification.

I am also familiar with what I call "epistemological terror". This is the anxiety and anguish that can be felt over the inability to know whether something terrible really happened or is a fantasy—and, contrary to some traditional psychoanalytic views, it *does* matter. It does matter to a patient's view of self, family, and wider relationships whether her father actually raped her or whether she fantasized that he did.

I have a patient whom I have been seeing for some years. Sometimes she produces material that seems to relate to ritual abuse, and indeed it seems plausible that she was subjected to this—yet neither of us has ever arrived at any conclusion about this. If we grasp the possibility that something terrible was witnessed or was done to the patient or participated in by the patient, and if this possibility begins to seem real to both participants, then we face the terror that both patient and therapist might be mistaken, caught up in a *folie à deux*; or if we lean towards the possibilities, on the other hand, that the images of terrible events are like dream images, bearing a metaphorical but not literal truth, and perhaps contain projections of the patient's own destructiveness, then our terror is that we may both be caught in a collusion to avoid the unbearable literal truth. The therapist walks a tightrope. Yet this metaphor is not entirely apt, implying as it does that he or she must stick to the straight and narrow and avoid falling into error. The therapist cannot just stay in some kind of central position of "neutrality"—to do so is not neutrality but a cop-out—but must help the patient explore the possibilities that are thrown up. Parts of the patient which are in terror may need encouragement to speak, may need indications that they will be heard and believed. An expression of seemingly neutral acceptance which covers private scepticism may be perceived by the patient as indicating not a safe emotional environment. The therapist is in an unenviable position here: if he or she does not believe the apparent recollection of trauma, the child parts of the patient will withdraw; if he or she believes the accounts, there could be dangers of colluding with a false memory. I believe that there are ways through this dilemma, but it is a difficult journey. It depends crucially upon not foreclosing the patient's own uncertainty; the patient who is uncertain may endeavour to undo this tension by eliciting *certainty* from the therapist.

The patient described above who produced images of ritual abuse without our having arrived at any conclusion about its meaning watched a television programme about a trial in the United States of a group of people who were accused of ritual abuse of children in their care. The programme clearly implied that the convictions were flawed because the evidence from the children was contaminated by suggestions from the therapists. The jury had apparently found this an exceptionally agonizing trial; some had become ill. The patient felt that the accused were guilty but also felt that the evidence was indeed contaminated. We talked about this as a metaphor for our struggle and ordeal in her therapy; within her mind, there was a prosecuting counsel that wanted to expose abuse, there was a part of her that felt guilty of a terrible crime, there was a defence that wanted to deny the accusation of abuse, a kind of internal false memory society, there were the child witnesses who needed help and encouragement, but whose evidence could then be said to be contaminated by suggestion—and then there was the jury, she and I, struggling to make sense of the evidence and the conflicting claims. Our only advantage is that we are not under pressure to arrive at a premature verdict. Truly, the tolerance of uncertainty is a most crucial and difficult discipline.

It might be argued that a courtroom is not an appropriate metaphor for the process of psychotherapy. But insofar as a court and a psychoanalysis are both attempting to arrive at the truth, then the analogy is apt, especially when criminal offences are being considered. Children and child parts of the adult patient do need to be helped to tell their story and to be listened to in order to recover—but in providing this help we run the risk of contaminating the evidence. In this and other ways, too, our work is inherently and unavoidably hazardous. Damned if we listen and damned if we do not, we can only endeavour to keep our minds (and those of our patients) open and try to hear and continue to think. Psychoanalytic work is a journey of exploration, through memory and fantasy in the fabric of the life cycle, as it interweaves inner and outer worlds. Searching for truth is at the heart of the analytic endeavour—the danger arises when we think we can find and possess the truth.

> Perhaps therapy can become the place where our pain is truly witnessed and our memories are appreciated, even celebrated, as ongoing, ever-changing interactions between imagination and history. [Loftus & Ketcham, 1994, p. 269]

(Suggested guidelines for psychotherapists in relation to memory are offered in Mollon, 1996b.)

CHAPTER ELEVEN

Recovered memories: shooting the messenger

Ashley Conway

In this chapter, Ashley Conway provides six of the commonest implicit or explicit assumptions that are made concerning false memory and provides research-based answers to them. He focuses on the issues relating to adults apparently recovering memory of episodes of childhood sexual abuse after a period of complete or partial amnesia.

T his brief chapter is a personal perspective, an attempt to identify and examine the allegations of the proponents of the concept of a false memory syndrome. It is not intended as a general review of the field. Issues of reliability of children's reports and suggestibility of children, which form an important and distinct field, are not addressed here. Instead, the focus is on the issues relating to adults apparently recovering memory of episodes of childhood sexual abuse, after a period of complete or partial amnesia. Individuals have reported recovering such memories both within and without a therapeutic setting.

Examined here are a number of assumptions, explicit or implicit, that have been derived from material provided by the American and British false memory syndrome movements, the press, and other media and through various personal communications to the author. The assumptions may be summarized as follows:

1. *One person can have pseudo-memories implanted by another person.*

    This is true. Memory is unreliable, and it is the case that people can have mistaken memories implanted or enhanced by another. However, there is a logical flaw that occurs repeatedly in the false memory syndrome message—because *some* people under *some* circumstances can have *some* memories implanted, there is an implicit assumption that where individuals and their alleged abusers disagree over "the truth", then the accuser's memory must be false. This is like arguing that because some women may falsely allege rape, then we should not believe allegations of rape in general.

2. *Because they are gullible, deluded, have axes to grind, or are greedy, therapists persuade clients to have false beliefs of having been sexually abused in childhood.*

    There is no evidence that anyone has ever had a false belief implanted that they were sexually abused as a child. Such evidence is not possible to acquire, as it is not possible to know for sure that a person has not been sexually abused, and it would not be ethical to conduct research attempting to implant such a belief. It may be the case that some therapists are gullible or hold incorrect beliefs. Yapko's much-quoted data (e.g. Yapko, 1994) shows that, of his surveyed therapists, 47 per cent believed that hypnosis improved *reliability* of recall, 54 per cent believed that patients could recall events as far back as birth, and 28 per cent believed that hypnosis could be used to recover memories of past lives. The first of these beliefs is a factual error, the second and third have little or no scientific evidence to support them. The false memory lobby implication is that if therapists believe these things, then they will believe in anything.

Some therapists may have axes to grind—some do have a particular belief that childhood sexual abuse (CSA) lies at the heart of many adult problems, and this preconception may indeed bias their approach. Of course it is also the case that many therapists and academics have preconceptions that child abuse is overstated, and that this creates in them a bias of denial of adults' reports of abuse. This is a frequent complaint of those trying to tell someone about their memories of abuse. Both child abuse specialists and false memory groups may contain individuals who have their own causes to advance. The false memory groups derive much of their energy (and presumably funds) from people accused of child abuse—so any difficulty that they might have in maintaining neutrality is, perhaps, unsurprising.

The final part of this assumption is that therapists stand to make themselves richer by persuading their clients that they have childhood abuse in their background and need prolonged and expensive therapy. My own experience, and that of colleagues to whom I have spoken, is that child abuse is actually not a good field to pursue if money is the main motivation. Victims of extreme childhood abuse are often dysfunctional, which is frequently associated with financial hardship. In the United Kingdom at least the situation seems to me to be the opposite of that which is alleged, and that in fact therapists frequently give a great deal of time and energy to working with people who have been abused for little reward or no payment at all.

3. *Hypnosis makes inaccuracies more likely and increases confidence in these inaccuracies.*

    It is sometimes true that hypnosis can be used to increase confidence in inaccurate memories. But it is also true that there is considerable evidence that hypnosis can also enhance *accurate* recall (e.g. Ewin, 1994; Nemiah, 1985). Again, the other side of the story is omitted by the false memory syndrome advocates. It would seem sensible to suggest that nothing about the truth *or falsehood* of hypnotically recovered memory can be assumed without corroborating evidence.

4. *A number of accusers have retracted, therefore accusations are unreliable.*

It is true that accusers have retracted, but this does not mean that accusations are unreliable. In its statement on memories of sexual abuse, the American Psychiatric Association (APA, 1993) reports that retracting can follow an initial report of childhood abuse in victims with *documented* abuse. One of the few studies on retracting suggests that this is frequently part of the disclosure process, and the retraction is often subsequently withdrawn and the accusation maintained (Gonzalez, Waterman, Kelly, McCord, & Oliveri, 1993).

5. *Having an explanation for one's problems by claiming child sexual abuse is an easy cop-out for the accusers—it means that they can blame someone else for their problems.*

The suggestion that alleging child abuse is an easy option has no foundation in reality—it is simply untrue. Coming to terms with childhood abuse is a long and painful process. On the other hand, it could be argued that denial is a much more comfortable (but perhaps ultimately less sane) option both for victims and for their families.

6. *There is no such thing as traumatic amnesia, repression, and therefore recovered memory, and greater levels of trauma are more likely to be remembered.*

It is clearly untrue that there is no such thing as traumatic amnesia. Inability to recall important aspects of a trauma is a diagnostic criterion for post-traumatic stress disorder and dissociative amnesia (*DSM IV*: APA, 1994). The issues of repression and recovered memory have been addressed in a number of studies. Herman and Schatzow (1987) studied 53 patients in childhood abuse survivor groups; 64% reported at least some degree of amnesia, and 9 out of 12 of the most violently abused women had experienced prolonged amnesia. Briere and Conte (1989) studied 468 subjects with self-reported childhood abuse histories; 60% reported amnesic episodes, with greater violence and death threats being associated with greater likelihood of amnesia. Cameron (1994) reported a study surveying 72 women in therapy to deal with the long-term effects of childhood abuse; she reported that "it was harder to find research participants who had always remembered their abuse than ones who had been at least partially amnesic to it". These studies involved subjects who were self-diagnosed and whose accounts were retrospective. Berliner and Williams (1994) cited a study by Widom and Morris involving a longitudinal follow-up of documented child abuse cases, which found a substantial proportion of the sample failing to recall the sexual abuse experience. A major prospective study has been reported by Williams (1994a), in which 129 female abuse victims were followed up an average of seventeen years after documented abuse. 38% did not recall the abusive event, and those who were assaulted by someone they knew were *more* likely to be amnesic. The evidence from these studies could be interpreted as providing empirical support for the existence of traumatic amnesia, repression, and recovered memory. It also specifically contradicts the assumption that greater trauma is more likely to be remembered, actually finding the opposite to be the case.

The demands of the position of the false memory syndrome groups are tricky: we are asked to believe that memory is unreliable, but in only one direction—that we can have false positive memories (we can be led to believe that something did happen, when in fact it did not), but not false negatives (we cannot apparently be amnesic about something that did happen), and that false memories can be implanted in adults by persuasive therapists, but not, apparently, in children by persuasive adults (see e.g. Marsden, 1994). Additionally, a claim of abuse is considered incredible, whereas a retraction by the same person is credible. When individuals re-accuse, do they become incredible again?

Both the American Psychiatric Association (APA, 1993) and the British Psychological Society (Morton et al., 1995) statements on recovered memories acknowledge the possibility of dissociative amnesia.

For a family to be destroyed by a false accusation of abuse is a terrible experience, and every effort should be made to avoid such an event. The false memory syndrome groups may therefore have something important to offer, but polarization (right/wrong, true/false) of highly complex issues does not help.

Academics in this field may be dealing with complex ethical issues, and those who have lent their names to these causes may become discouraged by this lack of rigour. The scare stories and one-sided anecdotes may be swallowed by a willing and gullible press, but if serious debate is to progress amongst academics and clinicians, then a much more scholarly attitude will be needed.

CHAPTER TWELVE

False memory syndrome— false therapy syndrome

R. D. Hinshelwood

In this chapter, R. D. Hinshelwood traces psychoanalytic theories on memory from Freud to the present day. He also provides a complex account of the interweaving in an analytic session between true and false memory of abuse. When, for example, is the memory of abuse a way of describing a present abusive therapy falsified as a past memory? More than anything else, this chapter highlights the multi-layered nature of a psychoanalytic session.

In this chapter, I discuss the question of whether we can know if a memory is true or false. In the first part, I trace the development of Freud's early ideas about memory through to contemporary psychoanalytic views on memory. I then move on to the complexities of abuse and whether a real distinction can be made between true and false memory of it. I shall have to conclude that it is too simple a question, the answer a complex one that is beyond the clear-cut verdict of a court of law.

Memory and its falsity

Psychoanalysis was founded on theories of memory, and these arose out of the prevailing school of associative psychology, in the nineteenth century. Freud developed a novel psychological theory, one that concerned the interference with memory. His views were based on an analogy with physical processes.

Psychic energy: Freud described associative processes in the mind as paralleling connectivity of nerve cells in the central nervous system. Both association psychology and the anatomical connections in the central nervous system were historical models even in Freud's time. He was not the only person to use the analogy, though most neurologists and psychiatrists approached the problem by looking at the physical brain (Jackson, 1931). Freud approached it from the psychological angle, though he was not the first to do it that way either. French psychiatrists, notably Charcot and Janet, had been interested in dissociated states of mind, in hysterics, and in multiple personalities. They investigated the structure of mind—its divisions and dissociations—and often the separate functions were correlated with physical protuberances on the head (phrenology).

Freud's originality was to go beyond this metaphorical structure of the mind and to develop a model that emphasized function as well. His model brought to the fore what he called "psychic energy", and he described psychological functioning in terms of the distribution of quantities of energy within the "structure"—within its divisions, functions, and dissociated parts (Freud, 1900a, 1950 [1895]). This addition was novel and was based on the emerging physics of electrical systems.[1] Mental functioning consisted, then, of the movement of energy through this whole set of functions and parts. The energy was discharged (like an electrical current) in various forms—through physical activity and, increasingly with the maturation of the person, through mental activity like imagining (fantasy) and thought.

Memory is a "system", a sort of black box that can become charged up with energy, or not, as the whole system determines. The associative links built up over time and laid down as a register in the neural network of the brain form the physical addendum to psychological functioning and development (Pribram & Gill, 1976). If a specific memory is connected with something on-going in the immediate life of the person, it is likely to attract some of the mental energy through associative pathways—and that specific memory will, now activated, appear in consciousness.

Repression

In the above scheme there is no theory of memory, there is only a metaphor. Yet memory was at the core of Freud's theories—or, rather, it is the *disturbances* of memory that were the core to his understanding of abnormal mental conditions. Freud's method was to understand the normal through investigating its abnormal deviations.

False positives and negatives: Disturbances result from distortions of the "flow" of psychic energy from one link to another. Freud noted that, on occasions, apparently, a link could become charged up but then fail to appear in consciousness, either as ideas or as actions. This is termed "repression". There is then a sense of tense, dammed-up energy. In some cases something else happens, an odd diversion of the energy: it finds unusual, abnormal, and pathological associative routes through which to discharge (Freud, 1900a). Thus two distortions of memory can occur: (1) repression, or the blanking off of memory which cannot appear in consciousness (e.g. the familiar experience of having something on the tip of the tongue); and (2) false memories, or a discharge into memories that are not closely associated with what is going on in the conscious aspects of the mind. In the latter, false memories may be constructed to create a confabulated reality or *déjà vu* experiences and other (more psychotic) phenomena.

So, memory is altered in two ways: through its apparent loss—that is, "negative" states of memory—or, alternatively, through the charging up of certain states of mind which leak out in memories that are not historical—that is, "positive" falsification of memories.

The role of trauma: Freud assigned a specific origin to these problems of memory. Impaired discharge of energy—its damming up or its inappropriate discharge—is a consequence of specific early sexual traumas. Trauma installs blocks in the associative links of the memory system, with subsequently an inappropriate alternative fate for the energy.

Originally (until about 1897) he thought that trauma was an actual *sexual interference* of the human infant at a stage when such an activity was developmentally inappropriate (Freud, 1950 [1895]). Over the course of evolutionary history, development of the human individual has become biologically attenuated compared with other mammals. The supremacy of intellectual development for long periods of childhood before puberty leaves a strange hiatus during which bodily sexuality causes stress in the child's unsuspecting mind and may be too much for it. That period of vulnerability opens the possibility of psychological stunting through a precocious sexual stimulation.

Conversion

Sexual activity conducted upon the child's passive body has an effect on his or her active psychology. This implies some conversion process from the bodily sensations to the psychological experience. It is further deduced that this conversion—from sensations to experience—must be a general phenomena involved in the creation of all memories. In fact, it is probably a process that is involved in the development of mind itself.[2] Freud described abnormal processes of conversion due to trauma, in which psychological experience is translated back to bodily sensations; he called these "conversion symptoms" (Freud, 1950 [1895]).

The internal world: Freud's recognition of the conversion process from body to mind directed him towards the processes of the "internal world"—the psychological perception of what is inside the body or inside the self. His view of trauma changed, too. As is well known, Freud came to realize that the traumatizing process is much more complicated. His early views on psychic energy were slowly supplanted by more truly psychological ideas.

He noted a difficulty. It seemed unlikely that there was so much deliberate sexual abuse of children going on. Instead of actual bodily abuse, he began to stress the psychological (or internal) component—the child's *imaginings* of what is happening to his body (known as "unconscious phantasy"[3]). So, within a few years Freud had relinquished the elegance of the simple sexual abuse theory of mental abnormalities in favour of trauma arising in the child's fantasy-life. The failure of his psychophysical model came hard on the heels of its invention. His stress on the body moved to an emphasis of the truly psychological.

Freud developed the conception of an internal world as a reality within the individual. It is where the young infant carries out the operations upon bodily experiences and stimuli to create a world of beliefs about what happens inside, and outside it. Then, increasingly, as the mind develops in the older child, this inner world operates upon the psychological stimuli (from the symbolic world). The conditions that form and distort this world of unconscious phantasy are greatly multiplied.

Psychic conflict

Trauma, then, was located as an internal event.[4] Freud adopted the idea of psychic conflict as the trauma to the mind. Two versions of this conflict were postulated: either (1) social mores are introduced into the individual during development and come in conflict with instinctual needs—a conflict between the superego and the id (Freud, 1923b)—or (2) there is an inherent conflict in all individuals between life-giving impulses and deathly ones, the so-called life- and death-instincts (Freud, 1920g).[5]

There are various outcomes to this trauma of internal conflict. The most straightforward is repression—contents of the mind that should be there just are not and have disappeared from conscious view. A second outcome is dissociation. Third is repetition.

Dissociated structures: Towards the end of his life, Freud came back, perhaps reluctantly, to reconsider the structural metaphor of the mind (Freud, 1940e [1938]). Having spent his career emphasizing energic functioning over structure, there seemed a point at which the dissociation of the mind into parts had become too neglected and so forced its way back into view.[6] Dissociation is now called "splitting". The core feature is that certain aspects of the self are completely disowned, lost—these aspects may be emotions, or they may be sets of ideas or memories; or they may be, more fundamentally, parts of the mind itself, such as cognition or perception. In any case, they involve inevitably important distortions of identity and personality. Sometimes this presents as quite separate but disconnected "personalities", inhabiting the same body, a phenomenon that had been of great interest to the French psychiatrists in the last century, who were interested in pathological mental structure.[7] In this case, the conflict was evaded by taking up quite separate points of view which never properly confronted each other. In Freud's example, a fetishist knows, in one part of his mind, about a woman's lack of a penis but, being so anxious about castration, he believes, in another part of his mind, that a woman does have a penis (Freud, 1940e [1938]).

Repetition: From very early in his discoveries, Freud was struck by another phenomenon that arose out of his clinical work, the transference. Patients formed a relationship within the analysis which replicated a relationship with another person and at another time, of a far earlier period of their development. The patient failed to recognize that he or she was repeating an unconscious pattern in his or her relationships. Certain features of the relationship between Freud and his patients held resemblances to the abusive relationship that seemed to have occurred with another person. In the Dora case (Freud, 1905e [1901]), the issue of an abuse enacted within the session led Freud to recognize the failure of the analysis because he represented the patient's abuser.

He was impressed by the re-enactment of the abuse (Freud, 1914g). It was clear to him that this was a kind of remembering, though not a conscious or verbal memory. Thus he contrasted two kinds of memory: firstly, conscious recollection; secondly, an unconscious repetition.[8]

Very much of the subsequent history of psychoanalysis has been a debate about the nature of the re-enactments in a psychoanalysis. The realization that patients repeat some very specific relationship in the treatment led to a concentration on the content of that relationship as well as on the energic economy that propelled it. The theory of psychoanalytic practice has become

correspondingly complex (Strachey, 1934) and has seriously increased the demand on the analyst's sensitivity to the interaction
between himself and his patient. The theory of transference was
developed and, more latterly, a new theory of countertransference
was created (Heimann, 1950). This immediate manifestation is referred to as the here-and-now situation. It is closely studied in
modern psychoanalysis as a direct means for understanding the
patient's past, and the ensuing trouble that he has in the present
(Casement, 1985; Joseph, 1975). Repetition in the psychoanalytic
session has become a key focus. It is now known as "acting-in" in
the transference.

The interpersonal mind

During the 1920s, there grew up a particular focus trained upon the
relationships with "objects". The specific psychophysics of mental
energy has tended to fall away—perhaps more readily in psychoanalysis in Britain than in the United States—and survives only as
a background in contemporary psychoanalytic discussion. The
emphasis that grew up in the 1920s and 1930s on relationships with
objects ensured that the new encounter with dissociated states of
mind after 1940 was accomplished with a dramatic change in the
way that dissociation was conceived. It has ensured that dissociation is now seen as having a deeply interpersonal aspect to it. The
structure of one mind is intimately linked with that of another. The
patient's internal world is profoundly moulded or constructed by
the immediate interpersonal context of the psychoanalyst's mind.

The development at the core of this strand of psychoanalysis in
the last fifty years is the realization that the mind can split up, and
parts of it appear, as it were, in the mind of someone else. In the
psychoanalytic setting, part of the analyst's experience may result
from an absent part of the patient. This kind of dissociation is
clearly linked back (through Fairbairn and Freud) to the nine-
teenth-century forms of psychotherapy associated with Janet and
others. But its new component is that the dissociation is effected
through the use of another mind as depository for the split-off part
of the subject's mind. The literature on this kind of splitting and
projection is now vast (Spillius, 1988). The patient's intense and

far-reaching relationship with the analyst, and the analyst's intense response, are now recognized as the key pointers to the
patient's current troubles. This relationship is of profound importance in probing the nature, veracity, and effects of abuse and the
(true or false) memory of it.

Privacy: negotiation or possession

I now turn from the development of psychoanalytic sensibility to
the nature of abuse.

The exposure to others of something private is always a risk.
The violation of the person is a condition of our time.[9] The sense of
the private turned inside-out to become a public arena is especially
focused on sensations of the genitals. It is not clear whether this is
inherent within the make-up of human anatomy and physiology,
or whether it is an experience constructed through the pressures of
contemporary social mores that has isolated sexual experience into
a category of its own. However, within our contemporary society,
sexual abuse carries, for all of us, a paradigm function for the
predicament of the person: it crystallizes the horror of this inside-
out experience.

The possession of one's own body is a highly sensitive issue.
From the beginning, the possession of a child's body (or that of a
baby) has to be negotiated between child and mother. The baby's
body is its own private world of sensations. However, that same
body is the mother's child, and she is charged with its care—
initially more or less a total care of it. Whose body is it? The two
have to negotiate this possession. Too great an exposure of the
child's world to the public attentions of mother and others is felt
as a severe intrusion—by one, at least, of the partners (baby). When
impinged upon, the boundary surrounding the baby's privacy
fades or is breached.

In taking possession of its body, the infant creates its private
world of psychological phantasy through the body/mind conversion. The internal domain of the mind is populated by figurative
phantasies felt as absolutely real. These, the patient's private possessions, are then "published" by the therapeutic process in the

"public" arena of the therapy setting. (I use the word "public" in the widest sense, referring to a setting that includes the presence of even only one other person. Hence, I intend to get the "public" quality of the baby's exposure with the mother.) Though the setting is only a microcosm, the intimacy and capacity for penetration can be as intense an exposure as any within the wider public space, if not more so. Unfortunately, despite the therapist's efforts, he or she may not be immune in this respect. Much of the efficacy of therapy is in the therapist's ability to contain the horror without himself or herself reacting as if abused by it.

However, the negotiated possession of the person in public is not all threat and horror. It can at the same time be a profoundly lifting and empowering experience. The performing arts, the fashion industry, publishing, and so forth are tributes to the allure of public life, both for the possessors and the possessed. But perhaps, also, in a category of its own, is the sexual opening and possessing of, and allowing of sexual possession by, another. In our culture at least, the pursuit of orgasm in the presence of another, with another, is what makes the world go round.

The horrific and the deeply satisfying are confusingly adjacent. These forms of public exposure are, psychoanalytically speaking, related to the successful negotiation between infant and mother over the respectful possession of the infant's body.

Therapy and publication

Returning to the arena of therapy: when a patient exposes part of his or her experience to a therapist the theory of splitting suggests that this can be more than just one person telling the other something intimate. A kind of psychological violation can occur. The patient can become a candidate for a potential added psychological abuse through emphatic interpretation or other forceful verbal activity by the therapist into the patient. We know, of course, that abuse by a therapist can then be acted-out physically as a sexual violation of physical boundaries between the participants in therapy (Jehu, 1994).

There is an important distinction to be made here. Actual physical abuse by a therapist upon the body of the patient is not

the only kind of abuse I am considering. The intrusion of the therapist's mind into the patient's can be abusive and can be suffused
with all the fear, threat, and horror of a physical abuse.

Now, it is not only this risk: there is another. We know that
therapy can equally involve the patient imposing on the privacy of
the therapist's mind. Any listener will react with horror to tales of
abuse and may become so filled up with the horror of the event
that that experience may become itself abusive for her or him—
even in therapy. In this sense, we have the familiar fact that the
abused repeat their abuse on others. Yet this is a cruel doctrine
when we take into account the dilemma that the abused has continually to mediate. He or she is barely in a condition to negotiate
satisfactorily with others the exposure of the private horror.[10] The
abused person needs to speak out but cannot do so without shocking the listener.

If one mind can intrude interpersonally with such force, then
therapy itself has the potential, it seems, to violate psychological
boundaries; ideally though, the therapy setting is free of these sorts
of impingements. Quite clearly there can be, and is, potential for
this psychological kind of abuse.

Speaking out: Like mother's possession of her baby's body, the
therapist's public possession of deeply personal knowledge can be
either negotiated and healing, or it can be unnegotiated and com-
pounding of the abuse. The loosening of the patient's boundary of
privacy poses a problem for the therapist. The therapist must face
whether he or she enters as healer or as violator. There is a balance
to be struck in entering the patient's mind which is comparable to
the one that the mother faces in possessing the baby's body.

The child gradually makes headway in bringing its experiences
into conscious thought through words. This process of maturation
is a key to understanding the problems in therapy: how much are
they brought into conscious verbal dialogue—talked about—and
how much are those transference situations silently and unconsciously enacted without end?

Repetition of some extraneous relationship transferred *into* the
relationship with the analyst is one form of memory. It suggests
that the act of memory is deeply public. When the extraordinary

processes of dissociation can "redistribute" parts of the participants' minds or their experiences within the therapeutic setting,
we have the ingredients for considerable confusion over whose
memories are being related or re-enacted. Once public in this way,
therapy attempts to alter the form of a memory—from enactment
to words. It is a version of the conversion process from bodily
sensations to psychological experience.

In fact the opportunity to talk is commonly understood as also
potentially healing: a problem shared is a problem halved. The
contact with another mind that can address and take into itself
some of the horror is a fact of therapy, and probably of the whole
field of human social intercourse in general. The experience contained within words rather than enactments is a staging post on
the route to a new negotiation of privacy and violation.[11] It is the
claim of psychoanalysis that the description of this experience of
abuse avoids the continuing enactment of it unconsciously.[12]

Abuse in the transference

This resolution of the past is not simple. It involves, in the transference, repeating experiences from the past—and that may be to
experience abuse. Interestingly, patients frequently comply in a
pushing, intruding exploration, which is a very interesting feature
of abuse, of sexual abuse—the familiar re-enactment of abuse—in
psychological form. The frequency of repetition has been noted as
a well-known response to trauma of every kind known, certainly
since the days of the First World War, when soldiers with "shell-
shock" or war neurosis exhibited both waking and sleeping
nightmares that continually recapitulated the traumas that they
had been through.

Working through: The understanding of transference implies the
offer of therapy as a public arena for working through those
evoked experiences in a conscious way. It is not enough that the
therapist avoids the subtle abuse of these psychological interactions; there is a curious requirement that they *have to be* worked
through in the here-and-now of the therapeutic situation. In other

words, the patient needs to re-experience the current situation as abusive in order to work through the past one! This raises peculiar issues. For instance, this requirement is not a recommendation for the therapist to become abusive in order to give that patient such an experience. Not at all. It is that the patient should have a living experience rather than merely talk about experiences. These are technical issues, but they also raise the fascinating point that the patient experiences the situation as abusive when it is not.

It is really difficult in the therapy session to decide whether verbal or psychological abuse is going on. The therapist may believe that he or she is not abusing the patient. It appears to be one person's word against another: the analyst may function in the therapy in a perfectly respectful way, yet the patient perceives a real abuse.

Abuse in phantasy: For instance, was Freud (1905e [1901]) an abuser of Dora when he seemed to press on her the unwelcome attentions of psychoanalysis? She certainly experienced them like an enactment of the unwelcome attentions pressed on her by her father's friend "Herr K"? (There is a wide-ranging debate about this in Lakoff & Coyne, 1993.) Or, was this a transference re-enactment of those traumatic sexual attentions? Freud certainly believed that it was a re-enactment—and it was this incident with Dora that led him to set out his ideas about transference more formally.

If it was a transference, it could be argued that Freud's actual conduct in the analysis is immaterial. The patient is trapped in her neurosis, forever to re-enact and re-experience a form of her abuse at a psychological, if not physical, level—whether she is, or is not, actually suffering another's abuse. Or, rather, the neurotic trap will remain until this can be converted into an expression in words and then the experience negotiated between the persons rather than possessed by the listener.

Yet it is somehow extremely important whether Dora did or did not actually suffer a further abuse, from Freud. There is somehow the uncomfortable sense that what Freud *actually did* was in some objective way over-pressing and at worst colluding with the abuse planned by Dora's father and "Herr K". In another instance, Princess Marie Bonaparte arranged, during the course of her analysis with Freud, to have her clitoris surgically repositioned nearer her vagina (Bertin, 1983). Was this a re-enactment of some abusive relationship stimulated in the course of her analytic relationship? Or was Freud in some actually collusive way partly responsible?

These are very difficult and uncomfortable questions, and, in a successful analysis, these kinds of complexities are what the partners analyse and thus bring into verbal expression.

False therapy: We know that a degree of coercion can go on in a therapy even though therapists should not push, press, or coerce the patient. Positive falsification of memory is an important factor here. In the effort to submit, the patient may falsify the current experience by displacing it into the past. In this case, a sense of abuse in the present therapy is denied by the patient—a process that may be happily assented to by the therapist—but then, like a *déjà vu* experience, adjudged to be a memory.

When the relations between abuse and neurosis were first debated, one hundred years ago, Freud's form of therapy simply recommended a method of releasing the unconscious memories which were blocked. There were at the time other forms of treatment based on suggestion and hypnosis (Janet, 1892: see Hinshelwood, 1991b); these recommended a more intrusive method—the modification of the patient's mind under the direction of the therapist. The therapist suggested new ideas, which he attempted to get the patient to accept. There was, here, a distinction between listening (Freud's method) as opposed to doing (the suggestive therapies). That distinction remains extremely important in contemporary psychotherapy. It is expressed in Wolf's distinction between "being-with" and "doing-to" (Wolf, 1971). This means that contemporary therapies that derive from hypnotic and suggestive methods are particularly problematic. Inserting suggestions into the patient's mind creates a real possibility of collusion in re-creating the patient's abuse in psychological form.

As I have argued, the risk of collusion is not absent from a psychoanalytic form of psychotherapy either. We have recognized the possibility of a re-created abuse; even the speaking-out in therapy can seem extremely exposing and equate with the opening up of bodily orifices. But the greater understanding of transference does allow a new leverage on getting a negotiation going rather than a repeated possession.

As the therapist–patient relationship has become more understood, through a century of practice of psychoanalysis, the distinction between verbal expression of the patient's mind and intrusive modification of it has become more intricate. These characteristics of the therapeutic setting are delicate, and they depend on what earlier in this chapter I called "negotiation". The paradigm is the distinction between the mother's intrusive possession of her infant's body and her respectful possession of it. The same subtle distinction appreciably affects the quality of therapy. The therapist's intrusive or respectful entry into the patient's world of experience is as delicate a distinction as a mother's intrusive or respectful attention to her baby's bodily orifices. Unfortunately, there are no objective parameters here. The only route is to meet, as openly as possible, the patient's perception of the therapist as one or the other—as intrusive possessor of the patient's privacy, or as negotiated respector of it—and to meet this in an increasingly verbal exchange.

Remembering abuse

If the therapy can, through the transference, be a false experience, how much more easily can a memory be falsified? The complexities reviewed here ensure that this is a problematic question.

What is really happening when, in therapy, a patient "remembers" an abuse in the past?

Crucially, the patient's experience is straightforward. The patient, rightly or wrongly, believes that the therapist is intruding into his or her mind. However, the therapist with a patient who reports abuse must bear in mind all the possibilities: (1) a repetition of a past trauma; (2) an experience evoked in the present by "invasive" therapy here-and-now researching inside the patient's mind and experienced as abusive therapy; (3) a present abusive therapy falsified as a past memory; (4) the memory of an experience already falsified years ago as abusive; or (5) some combination of these. (I have excluded the case where the re-experiencing is driven compulsively by an erotic satisfaction in being abused.) In practice, with a patient reporting in this way, the therapist needs to address the following issue: is he or she, in his or her manner of work, really impinging on the patient's privacy? This needs to be distinguished from the patient's need to express himself or herself through creating that experience in some kind of re-enactment in the therapy relationship. This is *the* crucial question. The experience of abuse in the moment of therapy can be disentangled by the patient from what is being recalled from the past. But no dogmatic rules apply, only the individual struggle to disentangle each case as it arises. It is a struggle in the present.

Conclusion: exposures

Exposure of secrets allows the therapist entry to the patient's private world. This entry can be intrusive—that is to say, the therapist, in an uninvited way, forces the exposure. However, without exposure there can be no help with the conversion process.

Conversion is, in essence, description. Verbal description, typically, contains in words what was previously overwhelming; and it is this that Freud stumbled on intuitively 100 years ago, the talking cure. In fact, it is, rather, the listening analyst giving words. Giving words to what is listened to contrasts with the suggestive therapies—giving words for the patient to listen to.

If memories become lived experiences again, to what extent is the therapist morally culpable for exposing the patient to suffering again? Psychoanalysts accept a necessary reliving in order to achieve a mutative working through, a containing redefinition, a verbal narrative formed from what has been inchoate. Allowing the patient to re-experience the past in a controlled setting is not the same—psychically or morally—as an actual violation of or intrusion into the patient's privacy. But both—the transference experience and a real experience of abuse—create experiences that feel the same to the patient. For the patient, certainly, the difference escapes him or her.

Finally, there is, therefore, a valid question: is "false" really false? Whatever is experienced appears always to be a representation of something or other. A "false" memory of the past can equally be a representation (distorted) of a true perception of the present (with an intrusive therapist) or a true memory of some event that was falsified in the past. This can only be assessed through recognizing truly how much the therapist conducts himself to allow only the expressive component of therapy, or reverts, deliberately or inadvertently, to a suggestive component.

The understanding of the dynamic properties of expressive therapy in the present is essential to disentangle the various possibilities. The complexities have accumulated into a bigger pile than we expected when we started. In all these, there is no falsity about the abuse—even though in some cases it might be falsely attributed to the past. What is experienced is a reality for the patient, even if it is only the reality of an evasion. That is still the reality of a falsehood. This is an alternative version of Freud's maxim that nothing is ever forgotten. Instead, we must recognize that no memory is truly false, only misplaced temporally.

NOTES

1. This model waned in popularity too, as physics and technology moved on to electronic systems rather than electrical ones. Electrical systems are concerned with the movement of *quantities* of electrical power, whereas electronic systems are concerned with the movement of small amounts of electrical *differences*— so-called information theory. Psychoanalysis has now tended to drop this early Freudian model; in fact, Freud himself never published his "Project" (1950 [1895]), which set out this neural/energetic model in most exact detail.

2. This process was later termed "alpha-function" by Bion (1962a).

3. This internal activity—working out psychic conflicts in the internal world—has come, over the course of the history of psychoanalytic thought, to be organized under the concept of phantasy: the mind operates upon sensations, creating mental experiences that are represented as figurative events occuring in relations with others—with "objects". Internal activities become, though, a private world of the mind, just as much as the body is a private possession.

4. Winnicott (1960) later returned specifically to external trauma. He referred to the "impingment" of the external world on the development of the sense of self, disrupting the "continuity of being" and leaving a falsity about the sense of oneself.

5. Turning his attention from the external world to the internal realities has brought recent attacks on Freud, because it seems to remove the attention from the wrongdoing of the abuser and place responsibility instead upon the internal processes of the abused (Crews, 1993; Masson, 1984).

6. Fairbairn (1940) also supported this return, arguing that the founding cases of psychoanalysis were those of hysterical dissociation, and that the trend following the work by Freud and Abraham on depression had moved the focus right off the structural metaphor. In the period 1935–1940, there was significant debate on the integration, or otherwise, of the mind (see, for instance, Glover, 1935). Melanie Klein later developed this return to structure in a way that has become particularly influential (Klein, 1946).

7. In those days, the professional interest in the phenomenon seemed to create a more general cultural pressure to which patients—most usually women, as it happened—responded by presenting more and more exaggerated cases that included the celebrated "multiple personalities". Some gained considerable fame and notoriety for their performances (Janet, 1892; Prince, 1906). Cultural pressures seem again to be leading to renewed interest in multiple personalities, with a matching response in the numbers of patients presenting themselves in this form.

8. Repetition may be conceived in terms of the energy model: the energy is redirected from the memory function to a function (activity) that is to do with the relationship in the immediate present.

9. That conclusion is at least suggested by contemporary preoccupations with "self". The narcissistic attentions to healing social wounds have been pointed out by Lasch (1979) and by many others (see Frosch, 1991; Richards, 1989).

10. The public arena, at least in contemporary society, is no sealed container for the chain reactions that can be set off. Where there is abuse, blame soon follows. The stage is set for an escalating social panic.

11. It is important to remember also that the story of abuse is itself a containing narrative, however flimsy the actual evidence—it can be containing for the patient but also for the therapist, when either is faced with the overwhelming.

12. However, can this verbal speaking-out in public, in therapy, be an abuse? Are therapists abusive in arranging a setting that is, in effect, a public arena for this private horror? Well, the answer is not simple—unfortunately—although Alice Miller (1985) and Jeffrey Masson (1984) do try to give simple answers and, understandably, they have their supporters for that.

CHAPTER THIRTEEN

How can we remember but be unable to recall? The complex functions of multi-modular memory

Mary Sue Moore

In this chapter, Mary Sue Moore reviews new research findings on multi-modular human memory systems which have important implications for understanding the impact of trauma on memory. She then focuses on procedural and declarative memory as shown in human-figure drawings.

Recent neurocognitive research has produced empirical findings regarding the non-linear organization and interactive complexity of all human brain functions. Previous methods used for measuring brain function—as *state* rather than dynamic *process*—have limited our conceptualization of the variability and overall capacity of the human mind. Theoretical formulations of these functions generally involved either cause-and-effect statements or attempted measurements of an "absolute" capacity. The most widely accepted methods of data analysis were linear. This chapter presents an invitation to the reader to consider the profound implications, for mental health treatment and human development, of non-linear, interactive formulations of human brain function which recognize *physiological process and context as dynamically linked aspects of an irreducible whole.* This understanding of brain function as a dynamic, interactive process, along with the concepts of neural plasticity and multi-modular organization, forms the basis of a revolutionary new theory of human memory.

The conceptual frame described above is one that relies on a complex systems point of view, not just as an option, but as a *necessity* if we are to gather an accurate understanding of any brain function. It has become clear that to adopt a linear, isolated frame of reference when analysing human brain function—in this case, memory—is to *distort* that which we are studying to the point of gathering "false or erroneous" data (Grigsby & Schneiders, 1991; Grigsby, Schneiders, & Kaye, 1991). Grigsby and Schneiders (1991) describe the *irreducible interactive whole*—which is comprised of the organism *and* its environment—lucidly arguing for the abandonment of the well-practiced experimental approach in which a particular function is selected and experiments are carefully (and artificially) designed to study this "uncontaminated" by other human processes:

> As Gollin has noted, behavior is "a function of organism and environment, and the proper way to study it is therefore to observe behavior in many organism-environment contexts" [Gollin, 1966, p. 3]. Given the organism's extreme sensitivity to contextual conditions, even *trivial* modifications of either external or internal environment will often have striking effects on behavioral outcome. Although not a new idea, this emphasis on the importance of contextual variability runs counter to the tendency in behavioral science, where the standard practice in effect has been to regard individuals (or brains) as the sole source of behavior. *Failure to consider the context may yield misleading or plainly inaccurate conclusions. . . .* [emphasis added]
>
> That living things are embedded in their context is, in practice, an aspect of reality often overlooked by both practitioners and researchers. Although one obviously cannot hope totally to understand the transactions of the organism in its environment, the arbitrary separation of organisms from their surroundings, which may simplify research design, is nonetheless erroneous. . . .
>
> Surviving successfully over time requires the adequate, automatic (and hence nonconscious) function of a number of

systems (modules) that mediate many factors: motivation, accurate perception of the environment, obtaining what is needed for survival, regulation and expression of sexual and aggressive impulses, formation of attachments to other individuals, organized initiation and completion of purposeful behavior, and the inhibition of irrelevant and inappropriate behavior. [Grigsby & Schneider, 1991, pp. 23–29]

The evolution of survival-related functions depends upon the capacity for accurate multi-level memory. If, in fact, we, as a species, were capable *only* of constructing false, inaccurate memories or of holding uniformly distorted knowledge in memory—not to mention "implanted" erroneous knowledge—survival beyond a few generations would be unlikely. Although we must be capable of "dissociating" various kinds of knowledge from our conscious awareness in order to develop the capacity for abstract, symbolic thinking, survival would be impossible if we were capable of forgetting our daily necessary life-sustaining functions.

Evolved memory capacities

Evolution has allowed humans to develop complex methods of perceiving, assimilating, and accommodating to change in ways that enhance the survival potential of individuals as well as the species. Inherent conflicts often arise between the dual evolutionary goals—survival of the individual and survival of the species—which co-exist but are not identical. Individuals perceive and respond to the environment in diverse ways related to genetic endowment and environmental impact on the developing organism. It is just this diversity that permits our species to survive changing conditions. Ironically, however, this particular species-protecting mechanism does not foster the survival of every *individual*, since individuals that respond in a rigid, specific way to the potential threat in the environment may not be well adapted to the eventual changes in the environment.

Consider what happens to a *population* when the environment is perceived as unpredictable and unsafe: innate physiological responses to the perception of threat compel individuals to act in self-protective ways (enhance survival). However, in an unknown or unpredictable environment they are forced to act "without knowing", an experience that is often accompanied by a state of anxiety. In chronic or extreme situations, this anxiety may intensify into a state of alarm or terror. The triggering of an alarm state is a neurological capacity in the human brain which causes certain changes in the blood flow, electrical potential, and intensity of activity in various regions of the brain. The physiological and psychological changes that occur in alarmed or frightened individuals have been well documented (Conway, 1994; van der Kolk & Greenberg, 1987). Pervasive, measurable consequences of such changes in quality and type of brain function include alterations in cognitive capacity, perceptual distortion, affective intensity, and responsivity of the alarmed individual (Grigsby, 1991; Udwin, 1991).

When an unpredictable, changing environment persists, individuals begin to function in a chronic state of physiological and mental alarm. This alteration in normal functioning produces measurable changes in brain development (Edelman, 1987; Grigsby & Schneiders, 1991; Grigsby et al., 1991) and predictable behavioural sequelae (Herman, 1992; Perry, 1993); however, the degree of external stimulation required to trigger an alarm state varies across individuals. Once the alarm–fear–terror continuum is triggered, physiological survival needs take precedence over psychological needs as innate survival responses are activated. This hierarchical response to the environment normally ensures that humans do not become so distracted by the "inner" world that they endanger their lives in the "real" world of physical needs and vulnerabilities.

What has all this to do with the "memory debate of the 1990s"? Perhaps a great deal. In fact, the best indication that the current "memory debate" has become related to our sense of survival is the fact that the discussions of human memory capacity frequently escalate to a level of affect intensity normally only triggered when we believe that our "life is under threat". How can we understand our defence of certain conceptualizations as though our lives depended on the outcome? I believe that more than an individual's academic identity is at risk here.

A crucial feature of our understanding of the world in which we live is our knowledge of ourselves. If we know our history, our capacity to function in certain situations, and our potential for resolving conflicts or crises in our lives, we have a certain level of confidence about dealing with the future. When we are uncertain of our own capacity, of our own history, and we are unable to predict what our responses may be to unexpected events, we are left exposed to extreme danger. Both psychological and physical threats then act as triggers for survival-related defences.

Learned *helplessness* responses (Seligman, 1975) and chronic unresolved mourning (Marris, 1974; Parkes, 1982) are commonly seen in individuals and cultures in cases where an experience of unavoidable traumatic loss has resulted in a learned response that there is "no way" to stop the pain, predict the future, or resolve conflicts. The normal assumptions made by members of a society—that the world is predictable and basically safe, that we can be agents on our own behalf, that we are capable of making positive changes in our environment—are shattered by experiences of unavoidable, life-threatening catastrophe (Janoff-Bulman, 1985).

In a rapidly changing and often alarming environment such as that of the 1990s, uncertainty, anxiety, and eventually fear can be triggered by the mere acceptance of the possibility that (as clinicians are telling us) aspects of human memory can be held totally out of awareness—completely unavailable to conscious verbal or visual image recall, but still with a powerful, controlling impact on our behaviours and interactions with others. The belief that we may not know ourselves—our capacities or our histories—tacitly undermines our sense of security by calling into question our competence to deal with the uncertainties of our future.

Selective exclusion: A normal defence against "knowing"

Bowlby (1980, 1988) has described the ways in which, when faced with just such a personal/environmental crisis, human minds can defensively engage in a type of *perceptual blocking* that allows the continued existence of a secure framework for understanding the environment and experience. This capability reduces the sense of confusion or alarm that we experience when confronted with information that, if taken in, would threaten our established sense of ourselves. He describes "selective exclusion"—a process that affects all aspects of our perceptual and cognitive functions, from the receiving of sensory perceptions, to the storing and retrieval of vital, related information regarding a specific situation. Bowlby (1985) states that "throughout a person's life he is engaged in excluding, or shutting out, a large proportion of all the information that is reaching him; secondly, that he does so only after its relevance to himself has been assessed; and thirdly that this process of selective exclusion is usually carried out without his being in any way aware of its happening" (p. 193). Once it is "selectively excluded", knowledge can remain inaccessible to recall for many years, only to be "remembered" when suddenly triggered by something in a later environment, or when the knowledge no longer threatens the security of the individual.

While current neuropsychological research substantiates the human capacity for selective exclusion, the concept was an unusual contribution when first proposed by Bowlby (Hamilton, 1985). Theories developed prior to the 1980s were generally limited to *linear* formulations of human development. Experiments were designed to discover "the cause" of symptoms (effects) that eluded comprehension. Specific efforts were made to isolate the human function under investigation so as to "eliminate any distortion or influence" resulting from any other source. Importantly, the computer—which can be used for simulation and to analyse massive amounts of information simultaneously coming from many sources—was not yet in use in biological research. With the development of the supercomputer, a vastly enhanced capacity for information gathering and analysis became available. New technology opened up the possibility for the observation and recording of *process* in human development.

Magnetic resonance imaging (MRI), positron emission tomography (PET), and ultrasound procedures have provided the means for relatively unintrusive monitoring of human physiological function in process. In terms of understanding brain function, the combination of the ability first to monitor multi-level physiological changes and then to use the power of a computer to analyse and model the complex, interactive processes has enabled us to glimpse the formerly unimaginable, dynamic complexity of normal human thought and perceptual processes.

A few researchers and clinicians have worked in the last ten to fifteen years to help create a language and a model for understanding the non-linear complexity of human brain function (Grigsby, 1991; Skarda & Freeman, 1990). It is to this framework that we must turn in order to integrate the knowledge of interactive process into a conceptual framework that clarifies and corrects the unavoidable distortions and inaccuracies of our previous linear, purposefully limited models of scientific experimental "accuracy".

Memory: conscious and unconscious/ declarative and non-declarative

We are increasingly understanding the multiple capacities for representation in human memory: case material from patients with documented traumatic histories (Sinason, 1994) is supported by neurocognitive research findings describing a multi-modular brain system that includes complex memory capacity in which verbal (declarative) knowledge and non-verbalizable (non-declarative) knowledge can be either connected or dissociated (Grigsby & Schneiders, 1991; Grigsby et al., 1991; Mishkin, 1992).

In a review of the literature on declarative and non-declarative memory systems, Squire (1992) offers the following definitions: "*Declarative* (or *explicit*) *memory* refers to memory for words, scenes, faces and stories. It is assessed by conventional tests of recall and recognition. It is a memory for facts and events" (p. 232). "*It can be brought to mind and content can be declared*" (Cohen & Squire, 1980). By contrast, *non-declarative* (including *procedural* and *implicit*) *memory* is utilized in "non-conscious" abilities. This type of knowledge is grouped within several subsystems in the brain— the subgroups only having in common the fact that the memories *cannot* be consciously accessed and verbalized. Examples of "non-declarative" learning are (1) the knowledge acquired during skill learning (motor skills, perceptual and cognitive skills); (2) habit formation; and (3) emotional learning or classical conditioning. In other words, *this knowledge is expressed through performance* rather than recollection (Squire, 1992, p. 233).

"Procedural" memory is one type of *non-declarative memory*, which records habit-forming and skill-learning experiences but is generally *not accessible* to verbal recall. In many instances, procedural and declarative (verbalizable) memory are linked—for example, knowing *that* you know how to play checkers and being able to tell someone else how to play is declarative knowledge, while the actual *interactive moving of the pieces* is associated procedural knowledge. However, under various circumstances, declarative and non-declarative memories of a certain experience may become complete dissociated (Cohen & Squire, 1980; Emde, Biringen, Clyman, & Oppenheim, 1991; Grigsby & Hartlaub, 1994).

A key feature of the various non-conscious mental processes is that "nondeclarative memory can support *long-lasting changes in performance following a single encounter*" (Squire, 1992). A single near-death experience, such as a near drowning or a serious car accident, can alter an individual's sense of self and behaviour for years—whether accessible to declarative memory or not. In most cases, the memory of the event will be part of one's procedural, non-declarative memory for a lifetime (Terr, 1994).

Procedural and declarative memory in human-figure drawings

There is evidence that procedural memory is fully functional even in early infancy (Hartman & Burgess, 1993; Tulving, 1991). A child of 4 or 5 years, without conscious memory of a traumatic, life-threatening experience in the first year of life, can accurately recreate the dynamic situation in play materials (Gaensbauer, 1993). A tendency to re-enact (Terr, 1990) or portray in drawings (Burgess & Hartman, 1993; Moore, 1994b) both unremembered and remembered early traumatic experience is well documented in research studying post-traumatic responses in children (Eth & Pynoos, 1994).

Traumatic experience can be held in declarative memory—whether related to illness, abuse, or other events—and these memories can be recalled, verbalized as well as represented in drawings (Goodwin, 1982; Wohl & Kaufman, 1985). In some cases, however, the interactive process or body memories of traumatic experience will be held in non-declarative memory—in procedural form—and any declarative memory of what occurred is dissociated. This dissociation of procedural and declarative memory may occur when the event involved intense traumatic affect, or when the individual was an infant or child at the time of the trauma (Moore, 1994a, 1994b). These non-declarative, procedural memories *cannot be articulated* verbally but will be evidenced in behaviour in specific ways, such as in habit formation. A child's drawing *process*, as well as the drawing itself, may reflect *specific non-declarative, procedural memories* of early childhood trauma.

This has obvious relevance for human personality organization, for conscious and unconscious self-perception, and, projectively, for the levels of self-knowledge reflected in drawings. Realizing that both lived experience and constructed meaning (including defences and coping strategies) are potentially being expressed in a drawing allows the psychotherapist to vary interpretive content appropriately, recognizing that non-symbolic representations may reflect memories that cannot be verbalized at present.

With careful study, we are increasing our understanding of the potential levels of representation in a drawing (Coates & Moore, 1997; Moore, 1990, 1994a, 1994b); however, no amount of study will result in the observer developing a method by which unerringly to identify or differentiate the many layers of meaning in another's drawing. Drawings are communications, and the interpretation of a drawing is not an objective science but an interactive process involving both viewer and artist. It is essential to remember that no observer—regardless of training, experience, or familiarity with the artist's history—can determine simply by looking at a drawing what each feature represents or means to the artist. We can, however be certain that a drawing includes many levels of meaning, reflective of knowledge held in multi-modular memory systems.

Human evolution, complex brain process, and the current "memory debate"

Multi-modular memory categories differ so greatly that it might be considered misleading to refer to them all using the same terminology—that is, "memories". In fact, the human brain has—precisely for reasons of adaptiveness in a changing and potentially dangerous environment—evolved diverse methods of perceiving and storing both declarative and procedural experience, not surprisingly in different regions of the brain. Brain-scan/computer-facilitated techniques such as PET and MRI now allow researchers to observe brain process in awake and active subjects. In a recent study, it was discovered that, when asked the same question, different individuals show distinct variations in patterns of brain activation while considering the problem. Since all subjects arrived at the *same correct* answer, had the highly divergent patterns of brain activity during problem solving not been monitored, this important individual diversity in process would not have been recognized (Ragland & Gur, 1995).

Differences in brain function in the processing of information are also revealed for gender in Gur's research. The complexities of the influence of hormones not only on brain development (from foetal states to adult years), but on brain process in an immediate task-by-task, day-by-day basis, can be observed and measured. In group studies, males and females generally activated different areas of the brain when answering a specific question, again despite the fact that all reached the correct answer (Ragland & Gur, 1995). This diversity in problem solving reflects well the complementarity of gender and individual differences and argues against there being a "best" way to process information, or a "superior" way in which to come to a decision. Since context is *part of the function*—not separate from it—divergent potential responses are more adaptive given a variety of potential contexts.

Technology allowing simultaneous access to brain process and the environment has produced the revolutionary understanding that physiological process and environment are an interactive whole that irreducibly *constitutes* the function. It is no longer possible to determine "what memory is" when we are simply measuring a single aspect of the process. The *context* within which we gather our "data" regarding memory *is part of the function of memory* (Grigsby & Schneiders, 1991). If we do not know who the subject is—what an individual's early experience has been, what his or her constitutional (genetic) givens are, what the meaning is to the subject of the presented stimuli—we can determine only a minute fraction of the given brain function that we seek to understand. We will produce "answers" that are not only limited in applicability, but also distorted and inaccurate as a basis for broader conclusions.

Current attempts to identify the limits of "human memory capacity" are severely constrained by the precise methods used to "measure" and the language used to elicit recall. Experiments with volunteer subjects who are asked to remember nonsense syllables in a laboratory give us some information about what can be recalled by a selected group of subjects, under specific laboratory conditions. The group results of these studies could *not* help us to anticipate or evaluate what a particular individual can recall and articulate of a previous traumatic experience, as the context and quality of memory activated would vary so dramatically. In addition, when one individual is asked, in separate environments or at different times and in different affective states, to recount the details of a specific event, he or she may recall slightly different material in each instance, precisely because *the context within which memories are retrieved is part of the memory itself* (Grigsby, 1991; Courtois, 1995; Sgroi, 1982). Perhaps our past inability to differentiate between and *label as different functions* these entirely different types of memory—each of which is an irreducible whole comprised of both physiological process and environmental context—has also fuelled the intensity of conflict in the current debate.

Some complications
to the study of memory in the 1990s

Having been carefully taught to ask questions that clarify complex issues by isolating one concept from another, we must now learn to avoid asking just such questions as "how reliable *is* memory"? *It is now abundantly clear that there is no one correct answer.* The *context*, the *precursors*, the *internal motivation* of the experimental subject, and the *affective state* of the individual at the time of the event *and* time of recall *all* influence performance on memory tasks in everyday situations as well as in the laboratory. However, evolutionary theory makes it clear that if all memories were "inaccurate" it would violate the dual "prime directives": survival of the individual and survival of the species.

In addition, when bridging the gap between research and clinical practice, it must always be remembered that using group results to evaluate an individual or a specific patient's responses is inappropriate. Research results generally compare the common characteristics of one group with the common characteristics of another group. In most cases, however, a number of individuals within each population will have characteristics that are unlike, or dissimilar to, those of the majority. The diversity of these individuals does not deny them group membership, in the same way that an individual patient's similarity or dissimilarity to a group profile only *predicts* group membership, it does not guarantee it. Applying memory research results to a single case is no exception.

Our capacity to observe and analyse brain function as a process is expanding at an incredible rate. We must assimilate new data into our "body of knowledge" on the subject at a rate that exceeds our ability to integrate it. This highly stressful environment for learning may be related to the continued tendency to return to simple, linear, absolute measurement questions and answers regarding the "reliability of human memory for early events".

The *need to know* is an aspect of human functioning that underlies many survival instincts: we need to be able to predict our own capacity to respond to crisis or life events, as much as we need to be able to predict what the environment will be like. "Not knowing" pushes us into a state of anxiety. In times of great stress, or threat, we make decisions of a dichotomous nature, usually related to taking one action or another. Deciding what is "true" allows us to experience a calmer inner state—less physically aroused and hypervigilant (capacities associated with the mid-brain and brainstem), more able to concentrate on thought and planning strategies (capacities associated with the frontal lobes and cortex). This polarized type of decision making is appropriate in emergency situations, but not when new theories and information are being presented and need to be considered critically in the light of what was known before. Conditions of anxiety are not conducive to careful, deliberative, integrative, abstract thinking.

We, within this book, are as caught within our historical frame as were any previous authors, and as we respond to our current context our thinking is likely to be unconsciously influenced by the exact elements that we are trying to articulate. New information about human memory does not fit into the old theories, but our current chaotic, unpredictable environment may be a factor in an increased sense of vulnerability that runs counter to the adaptive risk-taking involved when we take apart old frameworks in order to incorporate new knowledge. We may feel the urge to cling to what we have known as a way to survive and stabilize the turmoil of our current global, national, and local—political, social, economic—environments. By holding in mind the reality that our context is an inseparable aspect of who we are and what we are capable of doing, we might begin to find ways to counter the more unproductive, non-conscious, survival-related responses that may have fuelled destructive polarization and intense anger reflected in the "memory debate".

CHAPTER FOURTEEN

Objective fact
and psychological truth:
some thoughts
on "recovered memory"

Patrick Casement

In this chapter, Patrick Casement differentiates between provable objective fact and psychological truth, and between memory that has not been subjected to the processes of repression and memories that have. He focuses on these issues in connection with adult patients. Casement also deals with patients traumatized by complex family systems in which there is a sense of inappropriate sexuality and lack of containment but no clear evidence of actual concrete abuse.

I n this brief chapter, I emphasize the difference between objective fact, which is provable and which can be the concern of a courtroom, and psychological truth, which is the concern of a consulting-room. In particular, I wish to stress the distinction between "direct memory", which has not been subjected to the processes of repression, and "indirect memories" that have. To confuse these two kinds of memory, and these two kinds of truth, can be seriously misleading and may sometimes result in a patient imagining that there are grounds for litigation when there are not.

I am specifically concerned here with adult patients. I am not considering the quite different issues related to children who may be currently at risk and who may need to be removed to a place of safety. That is another serious matter but is beyond the scope of this chapter.

* * *

In *The Divided Self*, R. D. Laing (1960) gives an account of a girl who was regarded by her mother as mad because she was convinced that her mother was trying to poison her. The mother had denied this fiercely, protesting her innocence. Laing, however, listened to more than just the objective facts: he attended also to the psychological truth implied by the daughter's belief about her mother. He sensed, at a subjective level, that this daughter might have been in touch with some inner truth in her mother's feelings about her. Perhaps some sense of this was being expressed in the daughter's alleged "delusion".

The point of quoting this brief example is to highlight the different kinds of truth that are illustrated. If we look at it solely from an objective point of view, the issue can be reduced to that of asking whether the daughter's assertion about her mother was true or not true. If it were not true, then the daughter could be thought of as either bad for making a false accusation against her mother, or as mad in believing something to be true when it was not. But Laing pointed to a third possibility, that of finding a level of meaning in the seemingly meaningless assertion of the daughter. It may have been objectively false; but it could, simultaneously, have been subjectively true.

Laing could believe the psychological truth in the above example, but this must not be equated with saying that it described objective facts. It certainly falls far short of anything that could realistically stand up to legal examination. I therefore believe that much of the dispute that has arisen around the issue of "false memory", and the legal actions that have been taken on the basis of "recovered memory", has to do with these different levels of truth.

Let us briefly examine the status of "recovered memory". Memory that is recovered in analytic therapy refers to that which has surfaced from the unconscious *in the form of a memory*. But it certainly does not mean that this "memory" is necessarily accurate, let alone objective, even if it may have been based upon some actual experience.

When as therapists we are dealing with unconscious memory, or phantasy, we usually get a sense of what has been repressed through the derivatives that emanate from that which is still unconscious. In the case of a patient whose "memories" begin to appear in the shape of possible incest or sexual abuse, we may hear, for example, of a serious split between the parents. Frequently, we also hear of a mother who had been uninterested or too much absent. We may hear of a father to whom the child had turned instead for love and attention, for warmth and comfort. We may hear of a mother's frigidity and a father's uncontained sexuality. Along with this, we may hear of a father whose sexual interest in a child had been inappropriate. We may hear of sexual games between a parent and a child. We may also hear of a disregard for normal boundaries within the family. We may hear, in addition, of precocious sexual knowledge and even of specific sexual activity between a parent and a child. But when these details are based upon "recovered memory" (as distinct from direct memory) none of this can be used as evidence that what is being remembered could be proved to have taken place—and the law is only concerned with that which can be proved.

Even when the emerging details begin to present a familiar picture (that of a child who may have been sexually at risk), a therapist has to keep an open mind as to how this clinical material is to be understood. When we consider the family atmosphere in a patient's childhood, recovered "memories" do not in themselves verify any fact of incest or sexual abuse. They only raise the thought that this cannot be ruled out.

Now, when we think of the normal oedipal development of a child in a healthy family atmosphere, let us consider what is needed for this to be satisfactorily negotiated. It is an essential part of oedipal development that a child can, amongst other things, get affirmation from parents of a valid and healthy sense of his or her sexuality. Evidence is looked for to show that this has a recognizable impact on the parent/parents; that the child's sexuality is acknowledged and responded to positively, within safe limits and within a containing framework; and that the parents do not ignore the child's sexuality or treat it as bad (to be punished), as dangerous (to be run away from or to be avoided), or as irresistible and to be exploited.

Therefore, for a child to be able satisfactorily to negotiate the oedipal stage of development there needs to be a special kind of security provided by the parents. When this is available, it allows a child to be safely seductive and to have dreams or phantasies that may include some notion of seduction *by* a parent or *of* a parent, all within a context that allows the child also to return to an external reality in which this can be relied upon not to happen.

Thus, when a child is brought up in a family atmosphere that has allowed for containable phantasy, it is that safe atmosphere which enables the child to see phantasy for what it is and to know, eventually, that there is no real risk of these phantasies being literally enacted by a parent or parents. But when the atmosphere is not of a safe kind, when there is already a sense of uncontained and inappropriate sexuality emanating from a parent, then a child would not have a framework within which to discern, with sufficient confidence, phantasy from reality. A paper by Helen Resneck-Sannes (1995) is specifically relevant to the issues that I am addressing here. She states:

> There may be no actual incident of molestation; however, there may be sexual looks and comments by the parents toward the child. . . .
>
> The impact of growing up in an environment where the child is sexualised by one of the parents may leave the child acting and feeling like an incest survivor. But, there is no incident to ever be remembered. Of course, this is difficult for the mind to accept. It wants an incident to explain the intense unwanted feelings. [pp. 100–101]

Some children begin to develop a sense of seduction by a parent that reflects the psychological truth within the family. Similarly, some patients in analytic therapy develop a sense of having been the object of improper sexual attention from a parent. But this is not always supported by any direct memory. I think that it is then always important that the therapist should keep the options open, being careful not to come to any assumption as to the objective validity of these indirect memories.

I have seen a number of patients who had been clearly traumatized by the inappropriately sexual atmosphere of their childhood, because they could not rule out the possibility that what they dreamed of, or found to be represented in the form of "memories", might actually have happened. It is this uneasy sense—that these "memories" might contain some objective truth—that can lead to them being taken as more reliable than we should assume them to be.

So, if a patient comes to believe that there is objective truth represented in "recovered memory", it may be tempting to make accusations against a parent; but this course of action is fraught with many dangers. I therefore think that, when a patient becomes litigious on the basis of what has emerged in the course of therapy, this may reflect a failure in clinical caution on the part of the therapist. Instead, therapists should try to help patients, as far as possible, to come to terms with the distress represented in their "memories" *without* adding to this the further inevitable distress that follows from confrontation with a parent or parents. Experience suggests that more harm than good usually follows from these confrontations, however understandable the motives for wanting confrontation might be.

Some parents who have been accused of sexual abuse on the basis of "recovered memory" have been acquitted; some have retaliated by suing therapists. It is of course shocking to think that some parents who may actually have abused a child (or at least have contributed to an unsafe family atmosphere) could take retaliatory action in order to assert their innocence. But, because courts of law have to limit their concern to that which can be verified, some parents who are less than innocent will still be found "not guilty". By the same process, therapists who have been concerned for their patients, but who have not stayed with the clinical distinction between objective fact and psychological truth, are penalized.

The easiest options for a therapist faced by a patient's "recovered memories" are either to treat these as only internal-world phenomena (i.e. as phantasy) or to side too unquestioningly with the patient in believing these to be more factual than they may be. The most difficult, I think, is for a therapist to remain within the paradox of being prepared to believe the patient's own psychological truth as revealed in these "memories", whilst still not being able to know for certain quite what to make of what is being "remembered". Finally, let us also keep in mind that not all "direct" memories are objectively true, and that not all "recovered memories" are necessarily false.

APPENDIX:
USEFUL ADDRESSES

- *DAUGHTERS AND THEIR ALLIES (DATA)*
  PO Box 1EA, Newcastle Upon Tyne, NE99 1EA, UK

Daughters and Their Allies was launched in the northeast of England after false memory syndrome was fielded successfully for the first time in a British trial in the summer of 1994. A group of professionals, together with survivors of sexual abuse whose parents were members of the British False Memory Society, came together to campaign for justice for Fiona Reay, the first daughter in Britain whose father's defence team had mobilized false memory syndrome against her allegation that he raped her throughout her childhood. Ironically and tragically, Fiona Reay had never forgotten her abuse. She produced medical records that testified to a decade of trying to tell her story. Although the Crown Prosecution Service had initially assembled other witnesses and medical evidence, she was ultimately left as the only witness, despite their willingness to give evidence.

DATA is deeply concerned that members of the health and welfare system refused to allow their professional employees to speak in her defence once the accusation of false memory implanted by professionals was raised in the media. DATA exists to ensure that no lone survivor or professional will have to take sole responsibility for breaking the silence.

DATA is concerned that whereas silence is used by agencies to avoid this dangerous debate, yet it is mobilized by alleged abusers and their supporters as evidence of innocence, particularly when it is sustained by the accused parents' willingness to publicize their daughters' struggles without regard for confidentiality. Public health service organizations must not abandon their staff and consumers to stand alone in the face of a dangerous and organized campaign.

*   *ACCURACY ABOUT ABUSE (AAA)*
    PO Box 3125, London, NW3 5QB, UK
    tel: +44 0171 431 5339; Fax: +44 0171 433 3101

Marjorie Orr began Accuracy about Abuse when she realized that professionals were not appreciating the danger of the false memory bandwagon. Her newsletter provides latest research details and news.

Accuracy about Abuse (AAA) was formed in early 1994 with the primary aim of stemming the flow of misinformation in the media about "false memory syndrome", which it was believed would have damaging consequences for abused children in court and for adult survivors seeking treatment.

Backed by MIND, AAA was set up as an information networking system to inform media, legal, and political circles of the latest sexual abuse research and to provide the background to badly reported media controversies. Initially, the concentration was on material gained from adult therapy, though it has always been the intention to broaden the scope of the information sheets to include material more specific to children. It has grown in four years to an international mailing-list membership of over 1,000, mainly organizations, social work departments, therapy groups, lawyers, academic researchers, rape and incest crisis groups, and survivor groups. The networking of information is working particularly well at a national and international level. It has an outreach of considerably in excess of 10,000.

- *BRITISH FALSE MEMORY SOCIETY*
  Bradford on Avon, Wiltshire, BA15 INA, UK
  Tel: +44 01225 868682
  Director: Roger Scotford

The British False Memory Society produces regularly a twenty-page newsletter with a complicated mixture of more balanced scientific articles from professional members of its advisory group and other comments and reviews from some of its members. There is a problem here in that those parents who are wrongly accused of abuse do need an organization to support them. However, perhaps not surprisingly, the lay tone in the newsletter rarely shows a wish to understand why problems in the family led to such faulty allegations (where they were faulty) but more an untrained seizing of different professional snippets to caricature or "prove" their point.

- *THE FALSE MEMORY SYNDROME FOUNDATION*
  3401 Market Street, Suite 130, Philadelphia PA 19104, USA

REFERENCES AND BIBLIOGRAPHY

Abel, G., Mittelman, M., & Becker, J. (1985). Sexual offenders; results of assessment and recommendations for treatment. In B. Aron, S Hucker, & C. Webster (Eds.), *Clinical Criminology: The Assessment and Treatment of Clinical Behaviour*. Toronto: M7M Graphic.

Abraham, H. C., & Freud, E. L. (1965). *A Psychoanalytic Dialogue: The Letters of Sigmund Freud and Karl Abraham*. New York: Basic Books.

ACAP (1993). *Newsletter* (September/October). Bradford-on-Avon: Adult Children Accusing Parents.

Adshead, G. (1994). Looking for clues: a review of the literature on false allegations of sexual abuse. In: V. Sinason (Ed.), *Treating Survivors of Satanist Abuse*. London: Routledge.

American Psychological Association (1996). *Final Report of the Working Group on Investigation of Memories of Childhood Abuse*. Washington, DC.

APA (1993). *Statement on Memories of Sexual Abuse*. Washington, DC: American Psychiatric Association.

APA (1994). *Diagnostic and Statistical Manual of Mental Disorders—Fourth Edition*. Washington, DC: American Psychiatric Association.

Baker, A., & Duncan, S. (1985). Child sexual abuse: a study of the prevalence in Great Britain. *Child Abuse and Neglect*, 9: 457–467.

Barnier, A., & McConkey, K. (1992). Reports of real and false memories: the relevance of hypnosis, hypnotizeability and context of memory test. *Journal of Abnormal Psychology*, *101*: 521–527.

Baurmann, M. C. (1983). *Sexualitat, Gewalt und psychische* [Sexuality, violence and psychic impact]. Folgen, Wisebaden: Bundeskriminalamt, Forschungsreihe 15.

Becker, J., & Quinsey, V. (1993). Assessing suspected child molesters. *Child Abuse and Neglect*, *17*: 169–174.

Bentovim, A. (1992). *Trauma-Organized Systems—Physical and Sexual Abuse in Families*. London: Karnac Books.

Berliner, L., & Loftus, E. (1992). Sexual abuse accusations: desperately seeking reconciliation. *Journal of Interpersonal Violence*, *7*: 570–578.

Berliner, L., & Williams, L. M. (1994). Memories of child sexual abuse: a response to Lindsay and Read. *Applied Cognitive Psychology*, *8*: 379–387.

Bertin, C. (1983). *Marie Bonaparte: A Life*. London: Quartet.

Bertin, J., & Henifin, M. (1994). Science, law and the search for truth in the courtroom: Lessons from *Daubert vs. Merrell Dow*. *The Journal of Law, Medicine and Ethics*, *22*: 6–20.

Bick, E. (1986). Further considerations on the function of the skin in early object relations: findings from infant observation integrated into child and adult analysis. *British Journal of Psychotherapy*, *2* (4): 292–299.

Bickerton, D. (1997). *New York Times Book Review*, 26 January.

Bifulco, A., Brown, G., & Adler, Z. (1991). Early sexual abuse and clinical depression in adult life. *British Journal of Psychiatry*, *159*: 115–122.

Bifulco, A., Brown, G., & Harris, T. (1994). Childhood experience of care and abuse (CECA): a retrospective interview measure. *Journal of Child Psychology and Psychiatry*, *35*: 1419–1435.

Bion, W. R. (1959). Attacks on linking. *International Journal of Psychoanalysis*, *40*. Also in: *Second Thoughts*. London: Heinemann, 1967.

Bion, W. R. (1962a). *Learning from Experience*. London: Heinemann.

Bion, W. R. (1962b). A theory of thinking. *International Journal of Psychoanalysis*, *53*. Also in: *Second Thoughts*. London: Heinemann, 1967.

Bion, W. (1990). *Brazilian Lectures*. London: Karnac Books.

Blass, R. B., & Simon, B. (1994). The value of the historical perspective to contemporary psychoanalysis: Freud's "seduction hypothesis". *International Journal of Psycho-Analysis*, *75*: 677–694.

Boston, M., & Lush, D. (1994). Further considerations of methodology for evaluating psychoanalytic psychotherapy with children. *A.C.P. Journal*, *20* (2).

Boston, M., & Szur, R. (1983). *Psychotherapy with Severely Deprived Children*. London: Routledge.

Bowlby, J. (1980). *Attachment & Loss, Vol. III: Loss* (pp. 44–74). London: Basic Books.

Bowlby, J. (1985). The role of childhood experience in cognitive disturbance. In: M. Mahoney & A. Freeman (Eds.), *Cognition and Psychotherapy*. New York: Plenum.

Bowlby, J. (1988). On knowing what one is not supposed to know and feeling what one is not supposed to feel. In: *A Secure Base*. London: Basic Books.

Brewin, C., Andrews, B., & Gotlib, I. (1993). Psychopathology and early experience: a reappraisal of retrospective reports. *Psychological Bulletin, 113*: 82–98.

Briere, J. (1993). *Child Abuse Trauma* (p. 136). Newbury Park, CA: Sage.

Briere, J., & Conte, J. (1989). *Amnesia in Adults Molested as Children—Testing Theories of Repression*. Paper presented at the annual meeting of the American Psychological Association, New Orleans, LA.

Briere, J., & Conte, J. (1993). Self-reported amnesia for abuse in adults molested as children. *Journal of Traumatic Stress, 6*: 21–31.

Burgess, A., & Hartman, C. (1993). Children's drawings. *Child Abuse and Neglect, 17* (1): 161–168.

Butler, K. (1995). Did Daddy really do it? *Los Angeles Times*, 5 February.

Cameron, C. (1994). Veterans of a secret war—survivors of childhood sexual trauma compared to Vietnam war veterans with PTSD. *Journal of Interpersonal Violence, 9*: 117–132.

Campbell, B. (1995). Mind games. *Guardian Weekend*, 1 February, pp. 23–28.

Casement, P. (1985). *On Learning from the Patient*. London: Tavistock.

Ceci, S. J., & Bruck, M. (1993). Suggestibility of the child witness: a historical review and synthesis. *Psychological Bulletin, 113*: 403–439.

Ceci, S. J., & Loftus, E. F. (1994). "Memory work": a royal road to false memories? *Applied Cognitive Psychology, 8* (4): 351–365.

Cicchetti, D., & Tucker, D. (1994). Development and self-regulatory structures of the mind. *Developmental Psychopathology, 6*: 533–549.

Coates, S., & Moore, M. S. (1997). The complexity of early trauma: representation and transformation. *Psychoanalytic Inquiry, 17*: 286–231.

Cohen, J., & Squire, L. (1980). Preserved learning and retention of pattern-analyzing skill in amnesia: dissociation of knowing how and knowing that. *Science, 210*: 207–209.

Conway, A. (1994). Trance-formations of abuse. In: V. Sinason (Ed.), *Treating Survivors of Satanist Abuse*. London: Routledge.

Courtois, C. (1995). Scientist-practitioners and the delayed memory controversy: scientific standards and the need for collaboration. *Counselling Psychologist, 23* (2): 294–299. [ch13]

Crews, F. (1993). The unknown Freud. *New York Review of Books* (November 18): 55–65.

Crook, L. (1995). Letter. *Journal of Child Sexual Abuse, 4* (2): 115–118.

Davies, J., & Frawley, M. (1994). *Treating the Adult Survivor of Childhood Sexual Abuse. A Psychoanalytic Perspective.* New York: Basic Books.

Dickinson, E. (1863). *The Complete Poems of Emily Dickinson* (edited by Thomas H. Johnson). London: Faber and Faber, 1970.

Eastman, N. (1992). Psychiatric, psychological and legal models of man. *International Journal of Law and Psychiatry, 2*: 517.

Eberle, P., & Eberle, S. (1986). *The Abuse of Innocence.* Secausus, NY: Lyle Stuart.

Eberle, P., & Eberle, S. (1993). *The Politics of Child Abuse: The McMartin Preschool Trial.* Buffalo, NY: Prometheus.

Edelman, G. M. (1987). *Neural Darwinism: Theory of Neuronal Group Selection.* New York: Basic Books.

Emde, R., Biringen, Z., Clyman, R., & Oppenheim, D. (1991). The moral self of infancy: affective core and procedural knowledge. *Developmental Review, 11*: 251–270.

Erdelyi, M. H. (1970). Recovery of unavailable perceptual input. *Cognitive Psychology, 1*: 99–113.

Erdelyi, M. H. (1990). Repression, reconstruction, and defense: history and integration of the psychoanalytic and experimental frameworks. In Jerome L. Singer (Ed.), *Repression and Dissociation: Implications for Personality Theory, Psychopathology, and Health* (pp. 1–31). Chicago, IL: University of Chicago Press.

Erdelyi, M. H., & Goldberg, B. (1979). Let's not sweep repression under the rug: toward a cognitive psychology of repression. In John F. Kihlstrom & Frederick J. Evans (Eds.), *Functional Disorders of Memory* (pp. 355–402). Hillsdale, NJ: Lawrence Erlbaum Associates.

Erdelyi, M. H. , & Kleinbard, J. (1978). Has Ebbinghaus decayed with time? The growth of recall (hypermnesia) over days. *Journal of Experimental Psychology: Human Learning and Memory, 4*: 275–289.

Eth, S., & Pynoos, R. (1985). Children who witness the homicide of a parent. *Psychiatry: Interpersonal & Biological Processes, 57* (4): 287–306.

Ewin, D. (1994). Many memories retrieved with hypnosis are accurate. *American Journal of Clinical Hypnosis, 36*: 174–176.

Fairbairn, R. (1940). Schizoid factors in the personality. *Psycho-Analytic Studies of the Personality*. London: Routledge & Kegan Paul, 1952.

Faller, K. C. (1988). Criteria for judging the credibility of children's statements about their sexual abuse. *Child Welfare, 68*: 389–401.

Feldman-Summers, S., & Pope, K. S. (1994). The experience of "forgetting" childhood abuse: a national survey of psychologists. *Journal of Consulting and Clinical Psychology, 62*: 636–639.

Ferenczi, S. (1933). *The Clinical Diary of Sandor Ferenczi* (edited by J. Dupont). Cambridge, MA: Harvard University Press, 1988.

First Sight (1995). *False Memory Syndrome*. BBC2 television documentary, 16 February.

FMS (1993). *FMS Foundation Newsletter, Vol. 2* (No. 8). Philadelphia, PA: False Memory Syndrome Foundation.

Freud, S. (1893a) (with Breuer, J.). On the psychical mechanism of hysterical phenomena: preliminary communication. *Studies on Hysteria. S.E., 2*.

Freud, S. (1894a). The neuro-psychoses of defence. *S.E., 3*.

Freud, S. (1895d) (with Breuer, J.). *Studies on Hysteria. S.E., 2*.

Freud, S. (1900a). *Interpretation of Dreams. S.E., 4 and 5*.

Freud, S. (1905e [1901]). Fragment of an Analysis of a Case of Hysteria. *S.E., 7*.

Freud, S. (1906c). Psycho-analysis and the establishment of the facts in legal proceedings. *S.E., 9*.

Freud, S. (1909b). Analysis of a phobia in a five-year-old boy. *S.E., 10*.

Freud, S. (1910). Letter to Oskar Pfister, 10th January. In: Sigmund Freud & Oskar Pfister, *Psychoanalysis and Faith: The Letters of Sigmund Freud and Oskar Pfister* (edited by Heinrich Meng & Ernst L. Freud; trans. Eric Mosbacher). London: Hogarth Press and The Institute of Psycho-Analysis, 1963.

Freud, S. (1910c). *Leonardo da Vinci and a Memory of His Childhood. S.E., 11*.

Freud, S. (1913c). On beginning the treatment. *S.E., 12*.

Freud, S. (1914d). On the history of the psycho-analytic movement. *S.E., 14*.

Freud, S. (1914g). Remembering, repeating and working-through. *S.E., 12*.

Freud, S. (1915a). Observations on transference-love. *S.E., 12*.

Freud, S. (1915d). Repression. *S.E., 14*.

Freud, S. (1917e [1915]). Mourning and melancholia. *S.E., 14*.

Freud, S. (1918b [1914]). From the history of an infantile neurosis. *S.E., 17*.

Freud, S. (1920g). *Beyond the Pleasure Principle. S.E., 18*.

Freud, S. (1922c). Postscript to the "Analysis of a phobia in a five-year-old boy". *S.E., 10*.

Freud, S. (1923b). *The Ego and the Id. S.E., 19*.

Freud, S. (1924e). The loss of reality in neurosis and psychosis. *S.E., 19*.

Freud, S. (1926d [1925]). *Inhibitions, Symptoms and Anxiety. S.E., 20*.

Freud, S. (1927e). Fetishism. *S.E., 21*.

Freud, S. (1933a). *New Introductory Lectures.* Lecture XXX, Dreams and occultism. *S.E., 22*.

Freud, S. (1940e [1938]). Splitting of the ego in the process of defence. *S.E., 23*.

Freud, S. (1950 [1895]). A project for a scientific psychology. *S.E., 1*.

Freyd, J. (1993). Theoretical and personal perspectives on the delayed memory debate. Public Lecture, Ann Arbor (August). Reprinted in *Treating Abuse Today, 3* (5).

Freyd, J. (1996). *Betrayal Trauma: The Logic of Forgetting Childhood Abuse.* Camridge, MA: Harvard University Press.

Frosch, S. (1991). *Identity Crisis: Modernity, Psychoanalysis and the Self.* London: Macmillan.

Gaensbauer, E. (1993). "Memories of trauma in infancy." Paper given at the Colorado Psychiatric Society Conference on Post-Traumatic Stress Disorder, Vaill, CO (January).

Gaensbauer, T., & Siegel, C. (1995). Therapeutic approaches to PTSD in infants. *Infant Mental Health Journal, 16* (4): 292–305.

Geraci, J. (1993). Interview: Hollida Wakefield and Ralph Underwager. *Paidika, 3* (2): 2–12.

Geraci, J. (Ed.) (1997). *Dares to Speak: Historical and Contemporary Perspective on Boy-Love.* England: Gay Men's Press.

Glover, E. (1935). *The Birth of the Ego: A Nuclear Hypothesis.* London: Allen & Unwin.

Gollin, E. S. (1966). "An organism-oriented concept of development." Paper presented at meeting of the APA.

Gonzalez, L. S., Waterman, J., Kelly, R. J., McCord, J., & Oliveri, M. K. (1993). Children's patterns of disclosures and recantations of sexual and ritualistic abuse allegations in psychotherapy. *Child Abuse and Neglect, 17*: 281–289.

Goodwin, J. (1982). Use of drawings in evaluating children who may be incest victims. *Children and Youth Services Review, 4* (3): 269–278.

Goodyear-Smith, F. (1993). *First Do No Harm.* Auckland, New Zealand: Benton-Guy Publishing.

Grant, L. (1995). From here to uncertainty. *Guardian*, 16 January.

Greenacre, P. (1971). *Emotional Growth, Vol. 1.* New York: International Universities Press.

Greenberg, M. S., & van der Kolk, B. (1987). Retrieval and integration of traumatic memories with the "painting cure". In: B. van der Kolk, *Psychological Trauma.* Washington, DC: American Psychiatric Press.

Grigsby, J. (1991). Combat rush: phenomenology of central and autonomic arousal among war veterans with PTSD. *Psychotherapy, 28* (2): 354–363.

Grigsby J., & Hartlaub, G. H. (1994). Procedural learning and the development and stability of character. *Perceptual and Motor Skills, 79*: 355–370.

Grigsby, J., & Schneiders, J. (1991). Neuroscience, modularity and personality theory: conceptual foundations of a model of complex human functioning. *Psychiatry, 54*: 21–38.

Grigsby, J., Schneiders, J., & Kaye, K. (1991). Reality testing, the self and the brain as modular distributed systems. *Psychiatry, 54*: 39–54.

Gudjonsson, G. (1991). The effects of intelligence and memory on group differences in suggestibility and compliance. *Personality and Individual Differences, 13*: 503–505.

Gudjonsson, G. (1992). *The Psychology of Interrogations, Confessions and Testimony.* Chichester: John Wiley.

Haber, R. N., & Erdelyi, M. H. (1967). Emergence and recovery of initially unavailable perceptual material. *Journal of Verbal Learning and Verbal Behavior, 6*: 618–628.

Hale, R., & Sinason, V. (1994). Internal and external reality: establishing parameters (pp. 274–285). In V. Sinason (Ed.), *Treating Survivors of Satanist Abuse.* London: Routledge.

Hamilton, V. (1985). John Bowlby: an ethological basis for psychoanalysis. In J. Reppen (Ed.), *Beyond Freud.* Hillsdale, NJ: Analytic Press.

Hartman, C., & Burgess, A. (1993). Information processing of trauma. *Child Abuse and Neglect, 17*: 47–58.

Heimann, P. (1950). On counter-transference. *International Journal of Psycho-Analysis, 31*: 81–84.

Herman, J. L. (1981). *Father–Daughter Incest.* Cambridge, MA: Harvard University Press.

Herman, J. L. (1992). *Trauma and Recovery.* New York: Basic Books.

Herman, J. L., & Schatzow, E. (1987). Recovery and verification of memories of childhood sexual trauma. *Psychoanalytic Psychology, 4*: 1–14.

Hinshelwood, R. D. (1991a). Esther Bick. In: *A Dictionary of Kleinian Thought* (2nd edition, pp. 230–231). London: Free Association Books.

Hinshelwood, R. D. (1991b). Psychodynamic psychiatry before World War I. In: German Berrios & Hugh Freeman (Eds.), *150 Years of British Psychiatry 1841–1991*. London: Gaskell.

Hinshelwood, R. D. (1991c). Skin. In: *A Dictionary of Kleinian Thought* (2nd edition, pp. 426–430). London: Free Association Books.

Hollins, S., & Sinason V. (1993). *Jenny Speaks Out*. London: St Georges Hospital, Sovereign Series.

Hollins, S., & Sinason, V., (1994). *Bob Tells All*. London: St Georges Hospital, Sovereign Series.

Hollins, S., Sinason, V., & Boniface, J. (1995). *Going to Court*. London: St Georges Hospital, Sovereign Series & Voice.

Holmes, D. S. (1990). The evidence for repression: an examination of sixty years of research. In: Jerome L. Singer (Ed.), *Repression and Dissociation: Implications for Personality Theory, Psychopathology, and Health* (pp. 85–102). Chicago, IL: University of Chicago Press.

Home Office (1994). *Criminal Statistics, England and Wales, 1993*. Cm 2680. London: HMSO.

Hopper, E. (1995). A psychoanalytical theory of "drug addiction". *International Journal of Psycho-Analysis, 76* (6).

Hyde, C., Bentovim, A., & Monck, E. (1997). Some clinical and methodological implications of a treatment outcome study of sexually abused children. *Journal of Child Abuse and Neglect, 19*: 1387–1399.

Jackson, J. Hughlings (1931). *Selected Writings of John Hughlings Jackson*. London: Hodder and Stoughton.

Janet, P. (1892). *États mental des hystériques*. Paris: J. Rueff.

Janoff-Bulman, R. (1985). The aftermath of victimisation: rebuilding shattered assumptions. In: Cr. R. Figley (Ed.), *Trauma and Its Wake, Vol. 1*. New York: Brunner/Mazel.

Jehu, D. (Ed.) (1994). *Patients as Victims*. Chichester: Wiley.

Jones, B. P. (1993). Repression: the evolution of a psychoanalytic concept from the 1890's to the 1990's. *Journal of the American Psychoanalytic Association, 41*: 63–93.

Joseph, B. (1975). The patient who is difficult to reach. In P. L. Giovacchini (Ed.), *Tactics and Techiques in Psycho-Analytic Therapy, Vol. 2: Counter-Transference*. New York: Jason Aronson.

Kennedy, H., & Grubin, D. (1992). Patterns of denial in sex offenders. *Psychological Medicine, 22*: 191–196.

Klein, M. (1946). Notes on some schizoid mechanisms. In: *The Writings of Melanie Klein, Vol. 3.* London: Hogarth. Reprinted London: Karnac Books, 1993.

Kluft, R. (1990). Incest and subsequent victimisation: the case of therapist–patient sexual exploitation, with a description of the Sitting Duck syndrome. In: R. P. Kluft (Ed.), *Incest Related Syndromes of Adult Psychopathology.* Washington, DC: American Psychiatric Press.

Lacan, J. (1977). *Ecrits.* London: Tavistock.

Laing, R. D. (1960). *The Divided Self.* London: Tavistock.

Lakoff, R., & Coyne, J. (1993). *Father Knows Best: The Use and Abuse of Power in Freud's Case of "Dora".* New York: Teachers College Press.

Lamb, M. E. (1995). The investigation of child sexual abuse: an interdisciplinary census statement. *Journal of Child Sexual Abuse, 3:* 93–113.

Lasch, C. (1979). *The Culture of Narcissism.* New York: W. W. Norton.

Laurence, J. R., & Perry, C. (1983). Hypnotically created memory among highly hypnotisable subjects. *Science, 222:* 523–524.

Lawson, L., & Chaffin, M. (1992). False negatives in sexual abuse disclosure abuse interviews. *Journal of Interpersonal Violence, 7:* 532–542.

Lindsay, D. S., & Read, J. D. (1994). Psychotherapy and memories of childhood sexual abuse: a cognitive perspective. *Applied Cognitive Psychology, 8* (4): 281–338.

Loftus, E. (1981). Eye-witness testimony: psychological research and legal thought. In M. Tonry & N. Norris (Eds.), *Crime and Justice: An Annual Review of Research, Vol. 3* (pp. 105–151). Chicago, IL: University of Chicago Press.

Loftus, E. (1993). The reality of repressed memories. *American Psychologist, 48:* 518–537.

Loftus, E., Garry, M., & Feldman, J. (1994). Forgetting sexual trauma: what does it mean when 38% forget? *Journal of Consulting and Clinical Psychology, 62:* 1177–1181.

Loftus, E., & Ketcham, K. (1991). *Witness for the Defense.* New York: St. Martin's Press.

Loftus, E., & Ketcham, K. (1994). *The Myth of Repressed Memory: False Memories and Allegations of Sexual Abuse.* New York: St. Martin's Press.

Loftus, E., Polonsky, S., & Fullilove, M. (1994). Memories of childhood sexual abuse: remembering and repressing. *Psychology of Women Quarterly, 18:* 67–84.

Madison, P. (1956). Freud's concept of repression: a survey and attempted clarification. *International Journal of Psycho-Analysis, 37*: 75–81.

Madison, P. (1961). *Freud's Concept of Repression and Defense: Its Theoretical and Observational Language.* Minneapolis, MN: University of Minnesota Press.

Mancia, M. (1993). Love and death in the transference: the case of the Hungarian Poet Attila Jozsef. *A.P.P. Journal, 7* (3).

Mannerino, A. P., Cohen, J. A., Smith, J. A., & Moore-Mutily, S. (1992). Six and twelve month follow up of sexually abused girls. *Journal of Interpersonal Violence, 6*: 494–511.

Marris, P. (1974). *Loss and Change.* London: Routledge.

Marsden, B. (1994). False memory syndrome—true or false? *European Journal of Clinical Hypnosis: 48–55.*

Masson, J. (1984). *Freud: The Assault on Truth.* London: Faber & Faber; New York: Farrar, Strauss, Giroux.

Matasar, S. (1994). False memory syndrome and sexual abuse cases. *The Journal of Law, Medicine and Ethics, 22*: 286–288.

Mawby, R., & Walklate, S. (1994). *Critical Victimology.* London: Sage.

Miller, A. (1985). *Thou Shalt Not Be Aware: Society's Betrayal of the Child.* London: Pluto.

Milton, J. (1994). Abuser and abuse. *A.P.P. Journal, 8* (3).

Mishkin, M. (1992). Cerebral memory circuits. In: T. A. Poggio & D. A. Glaser (Eds.), *Exploring Brain Functions: Models in Neuroscience.* New York: Wiley.

Mollon, P. (1995). Clinical psychologists, recovered memory and false memory. *Clinical Psychology Forum, 86* (December): 17–20.

Mollon, P. (1996a). *Multiple Selves, Multiple Voices. Working with Trauma, Violation and Dissociation.* London: Wiley.

Mollon, P. (1996b). The memory debate: a consideration of some clinical complexities and some suggested guidelines for psychoanalytic therapists. *British Journal of Psychotherapy, 13* (2): 193–203.

Mollon, P. (1998). *Remembering Trauma: A Psychotherapist's Guide to Memory and Illusion.* Chichester: Wiley.

Moore, M. S. (1990). Understanding children's drawings: developmental and emotional indicators in children's human figure drawings. *Journal of Educational Therapy, 3*: 35–47.

Moore, M. S. (1994a). Common characteristics in the human figure drawings of ritually abused children and adults. In: V. Sinason (Ed.), *Treating Survivors of Satanist Abuse.* London: Routledge.

Moore, M. S. (1994b). Reflections of self: drawings of children with physical Illness. In: A. Erskine & D. Judd (Eds.), *The Imaginative Body: Psychodynamic Therapy in Health Care.* London: Whurr.

Morton, J., Andrews, B., Brewin, C., Davies, G., & Mollon, P. (1995). *Recovered Memories: The Report of the Working Party of the British Psychological Society*. Leicester: British Psychological Society.

Mullen, P. E., Romans, S. E., Walton, V. A., & Herbison, G. P. (1988). Impact of sexual and physical abuse on women's mental health. *Lancet* (i): 841–845.

Mullen, P., Martin, J., Anderson, J., Romans, S., & Herbison, G. (1993). Child sexual abuse and mental health in later life. *British Journal of Psychiatry, 163*: 721–730.

Murrey, G., Cross, H., & Whipple, J. (1992). Hypnotically created pseudo-memories: further investigation into the " Memory distortion or Response Bias question". *Journal of Abnormal Psychology, 101*: 75–77.

Nemiah, J. C. (1985). Dissociative disorders (hysterical neurosis, dissociative type). In: H. I. Kaplan & B. J. Sadock (Eds), *Comprehensive Textbook of Psychiatry* (4th edition). Baltimore: Williams & Wilkins.

Ofshe, R., & Watters, E. (1994). *Making Monsters: False Memories, Psychotherapy and Sexual Hysteria*. New York: Scribners.

Orne, T. (1979). The use and misuse of hypnosis in the courtroom. *International Journal of Clinical and Experimental Hypnosis, 27*: 331–347.

Parkes, C. M. (1982). Attachment and the prevention of mental disorders. In: C. M. Parkes & J. Stevenson-Hinde (Eds.), *The Place of Attachment in Human Behavior*. New York: Basic Books.

Parkes, C. M., & Stevenson-Hinde, J. (Eds.) (1982). *The Place of Attachment in Human Behavior*. New York: Basic Books.

Pendergrast, M. (1994). *Victims of Memory: Incest Accusations and Shattered Lives*. Hinesburg, VT: Upper Access.

Perry, B. (1993). Neurodevelopment and the neurophysiology of trauma, I and II. *The Advisor, Journal of the American Professional Society on the Abuse of Children, 6*.

Perry, B., Pollard, R., Blakley, T., Baker, W., & Vigilante, D. (1995). Childhood trauma, the neurobiology of adaptation and "use-dependent" development of the brain: how "states" become "traits". *Infant Mental Health Journal, 16* (4): 271.

Pope, H. G., Jr., & Hudson, J. I. (1995). Can memories of childhood sexual abuse be repressed? *Psychological Medicine, 25*: 121–126.

Pope, K. S. (1996). Memory, abuse, and science: questioning claims about the false memory syndrome. *American Psychologist, 51* (9): 957–974.

Pribram, K., & Gill, M. (1976). *Freud's "Project" Reassessed*. London: Hutchinson.

Prince, M. (1906). *The Dissociation of a Personality*. New York: Longmans.

Putnam, F. (1985). Dissociation as a response to extreme trauma. In: R. Kluff (Ed.), *Childhood Antecedents of Multiple Personality Disorder*. Washington, DC: American Psychiatric Press.

Ragland, J. D., & Gur, R.-C. (1995). Reliability and construct validity of the Paired Associate Recognition Test: a test of declarative memory using Wisconsin Card-sorting Stimuli. *Psychological Assessment, 7* (1): 25–32.

Reder, P., & Duncan, S. (1993). Closure, covert warnings and escalating child abuse. *Child Abuse and Neglect, 19* (12): 1517–1521.

Resneck-Sannes, H. (1995). A feeling in search of a memory. *Women & Therapy, 16* (4): 97–105.

Rey, H. (1986). The psychodynamics of psychoanalytic and psycholinguistic structures. In: *Universals of Psychoanalysis in the Treatment of Psychotic and Borderline States: Factors of Space–Time and Language* (pp. 176–189), edited by J. Magagna. London: Free Association Books, 1994.

Rey, H. (1994). *Universals of Psychoanalysis in the Treatment of Psychotic and Borderline States: Factors of Space–Time and Language*, edited by J. Magagna. London: Free Association Books.

Rhode, E. (1994). *Psychotic Metaphysics*. London: Karnac Books.

Richards, B. (Ed.) (1989). *Crises of the Self: Further Essays on Psychoanalysis and Politics*. London: Free Association Books.

Rosenfeld, H. (1971). A clinical approach to the psychoanalytic theory of the life and death instincts. *International Journal of Psychoanalysis, 52*.

Salter, A. (1991). Accuracy of expert testimony in child sexual abuse cases. A case study of Ralph Underwager and Hollida Wakefield. Unpublished manuscript on file with the American Prosecutors Research Institute, National Center for Prosecution of Child Abuse (Alexandria, VA).

Sandfort, T. (1983). Pedophile relationships in Netherlands: alternative lifestyle for children? *Alternative Lifestyles, 5* (Spring, 3): 164–183.

Saywitz, K., Goodman, G., Nicholas, E., & Moan, S. (1991). Children's memories of a physical examination involving genital touch: implications for reports of child sexual abuse. *Journal of Consulting and Clinical Psychology 59* (October, 5): 682–691.

Schooler, J. W. (1994). Seeking the core: the issues and evidence surrounding recovered accounts of sexual trauma. *Consciousness and Cognition, 3*: 452–469.

Searle, J. (1969). *Speech Acts: An Essay in the Philosophy of Language.* New York: Cambridge University Press.

Segal, H. (1986). *The Work of Hanna Segal.* London: Free Association Books.

Segal, H. (1981). *The Work of Hannah Segal: A Kleinian Approach to Clinical Practice.* Northvale, NJ: Jason Aronson. [Reprinted London: Karnac Books, 1988.]

Segal, H. (1991). *Dream, Phantasy and Art.* London: Routledge.

Seligman, M. (1975). *Learned Helplessness.* San Francisco, CA: Freeman.

Sgroi, S. (1982). *Handbook of Clinical Intervention in Child Sexual Abuse.* Toronto: Lexington Books.

Sgroi, S. (1989). *Vulnerable Populations, Vol. 1.* Lexington, MA: Lexington Books.

Sheehan, P., Statham, D., & Jamieson, G. (1991). Pseudo-memory effects and their relationship to level of susceptibility to hypnosis and state instruction. *Journal of Personality and Social Psychology, 60:* 130–137.

Simon, B. (1992). "Incest—see under Oedipus Complex": the history of an error in psychoanalysis. *Journal of the American Psychoanalytic Association, 40* (4): 955–988.

Sinason, M. (1993). Who is the mad voice inside? *A.P.P. Journal, 7* (3).

Sinason, V. (1993). *Mental Handicap and the Human Condition.* London: Free Association Books.

Sinason, V. (Ed.) (1994). *Treating Survivors of Satanist Abuse.* London: Routledge.

Sinason, V. (1997). Remembering in therapy. In: J. Sandler (Ed.), *Recovered Memories of Abuse: True or False?* London: Karnac Books, 1997.

Skarda, A., & Freeman, W. (1990). Representations: who needs them. In: J. L. McGough & N. Weinberger (Eds.), *Brain Organization and Memory: Cells, Systems, and Circuits* (pp. 375–380). New York: Oxford University Press.

Sorenson, T., & Snow, B. (1991). How children tell: the process of disclosure of sexual abuse. *Child Welfare, 70:* 3–15.

Spanos, N. P., Gwynn, M. I., Comer, S. L., Baltruwiet, W., & de Groh, M. (1989). Are hypnotically induced memories resistant to cross examination? *Law and Human Behaviour, 13:* 271–289.

Spillius, E. (1988). *Melanie Klein Today* (2 vols). London: Routledge.

Squire, L. (1992). Declarative and nondeclarative memory: multiple brain systems supporting learning and memory. *Journal of Cognitive Neuroscience, 4* (3): 232–243.

Steiner, J. (1993). *Psychic Retreats.* London: Routledge.

Stern, D. (1993). Acting versus remembering and transference love and infantile love. In: E. Person, A. Hagelin, & P. Fonagy (Eds.), *On Freud's "Observations on Transference-Love"* (pp. 172–185). New Haven, CT: Yale University Press.

Strachey, J. (1934). The nature of the therapeutic action of psychoanalysis. *International Journal of Psycho-Analysis, 15*: 127–159.

Summit, R. C. (1983). The child sexual abuse accommodation syndrome. *Child Abuse and Neglect, 7*: 177–193.

Szur, R., & Miller, S. (1992). *Extending Horizons: Psychoanalytic Psychotherapy with children, Adolescents and Families.* London: Karnac Books.

Terr, L. (1990). *Too Scared to Cry.* New York: Harper & Row.

Terr, L. (1991). Childhood traumas: an outline and overview. *American Journal of Psychiatry, 148*: 10–20.

Terr, L. (1994). *Unchained Memories. True Stories of Traumatic Memories Lost and Found.* New York: Basic Books.

Terri, W. (1991). Perpetrator and victim accounts of sexual abuse (paper presented at The Health Science Response to Child Maltreatment, Centre for Child Protection, San Diego). In: K. C. Faller (1994), Commentary on the children forgotten in the Inter-Disciplinary Census Statement. *Journal of Child Sexual Abuse, 3*: 115–121.

Trepper, T., & Barrett, M. J. (1989). *Systemic Treatment of Incest: A Therapeutic Handbook.* New York: Hayworth.

Trowell, J. (1986). Physical abuse of children: some considerations seen from the dynamic perspective. *Psychoanalytic Psychotherapy, 2*: 63–73.

Tulving, E. (1991). Interview with Eindold. *Journal of Cognitive Neuro-Science, 3*: 89.

Tyrrell, I. (1994). Untitled (review of *First Do No Harm*). *BFMS Newsletter, 2* (3) (10 December).

Udwin, O. (1991). Screening child survivors for PTSD: experiences from the *Jupiter* sinking. *British Journal of Clinical Psychology, 30* (2): 131–138.

Ulman, R. B., & Brothers, D. (1988). *The Shattered Self. A Psychoanalytic Study of Trauma.* Hillsdale, NJ: Analytic Press.

Underwager, R., & Wakefield, H. (1990). *The Real World of Child Interrogations.* Springfield, IL: Charles C Thomas.

van der Kolk, B. (Ed.) (1987). *Psychological Trauma.* Washington, DC: American Psychiatric Press.

van der Kolk, B. (1994). The minefields of memory. *Boston Globe Book Review* (Nov. 10): B21–22.

van der Kolk, B. (1996). Trauma and memory. In B. van der Kolk, A.C.

McFarlane, & L. Weisaeth (Eds.), *Traumatic Stress*. New York: Guilford Press.

van der Kolk, B., & Greenberg, M. (1987). The psychobiology of the trauma response: hyperarousal, constriction, and addiction to traumatic re-exposure. In: B. van der Kolk (Ed.), *Psychological Trauma*. Washington, DC: American Psychiatric Press.

van der Kolk, B., & Saporta, J. (1993). Biological responses to psychic trauma. In: J. Wilson & B. Raphael (Eds.), *International Handbook of Traumatic Stress Syndromes*. New York: Plenum.

Van Leeuwen, K. (1988). Resistances in the treatment of a sexually molested 6-year-old girl. *International Review of Psycho-Analysis*, 15 (2): 149–156.

Vizard, E. (1988). Child sexual abuse—the child's experience. *British Journal of Psychotherapy*, 5 (1): 77–91.

Wakefield, H., & Underwager, R. (1988). *Accusations of Child Sexual Abuse*. Springfield, IL: Charles C Thomas.

Walmsley, R., & White, K. (1979). *Sexual Offences, Consent and Sentencing. Home Office Research Study, No. 54*. Home Office Research Unit. London: HMSO.

Williams, L. M. (1992). Adult memories of childhood abuse. *The Advisor, Journal of the American Professional Society on the Abuse of Children*, 5: 19–21.

Williams, L. M. (1994a) Recall of childhood trauma: a prospective study of women's memories of child sexual abuse. *Journal of Consulting and Clinical Psychology*, 62: 1167–1176.

Williams, L. M. (1994b). What does it mean to forget child sexual abuse? A reply to Loftus, Garry, and Feldman (1994). *Journal of Consulting and Clinical Psychology*, 62: 1182–1186.

Williams, L. M. (1995). Recovered memories of abuse in women with documented child sexual victimization histories. *Journal of Traumatic Stress*, 8: 649–673.

Winnicott, D. W. (1960). *The Maturational Processes and the Facilitating Environment*. London: Hogarth. Reprinted London: Karnac Books, 1990.

Winnicott, D. W. (1960). The theory of the parent–infant relationship. *International Journal of Psycho-Analysis*, 41: 585–595.

Wiseman, M. R., Vizard, E., Bentovim, A., & Leventhal, J. (1992). Reliability of videotaped interviews with children suspected of being sexually abused. *British Medical Journal*. 304: 1089–1091.

Wohl, A., & Kaufman, B. (1985). *Silent Screams & Hidden Cries: An Interpretation of Artwork by Children from Violent Homes*. New York: Brunner/Mazel.

Wolf, H. (1971). The therapeutic and development functions of psychotherapy. *British Journal of Medical Psychology*, 44: 117–130.

Yapko, M. D. (1994). Suggestibility and repressed memories of abuse: a survey of psychotherapist's beliefs. *American Journal of Clinical Hypnosis*, 36: 163–171.

With thanks to Angela Hazelton, Tavistock Library, for her assistance.

INDEX

Abel, G., 25
Abraham, K., 128, 165
abuse (*passim*):
   nature of, 156–163
   see also: child abuse; denial
Accommodation Syndrome
   [Summit], 36
Accuracy about Abuse (AAA), 85,
   92, 186
acting out, 69, 102, 115, 119
   vs. remembering, 111–112, 117
Adler, Z., 18
Adshead, G., ix, 4, 8, 9, 10, 17–27,
   98
age-associated memory deficit, 120
aggressor, identification with: *see*
   identification, with
   aggressor
alarm state, physiological and
   psychological effects of, 169
alpha-function [Bion], 164
American Psychiatric Association,
   7, 146, 147

American Psychological
   Association, 135
amnesia, 58, 83
   dissociative, 146, 147
   infantile, 12
   and memory mechanisms,
     130–135
   motivated, in response to trauma,
     135
   total, memory recovery from, 4,
     143–148
   traumatic, 22, 146–147
Anderson, J., 22
Andrews, B., 4, 6, 22
Association of Child
   Psychotherapists, 108
attachment:
   to family, loss of, 19
   research, 5
attention-deficit disorder (ADD),
   120

Bacon, F., 17

205